Claiming Citizenship

NUMBER THREE:

Fronteras Series
Sponsored by Texas A&M International University
José Roberto Juárez
General Editor

CLAIMING

Mexican Americans

CITIZENSHIP

in Victoria, Texas

Anthony Quiroz

Texas A&M University Press
College Station

The paper used in this book meets the minimum requirements
of the American National Standard for Permanence
of Paper for Printed Library Materials, z39.48-1984.
Binding materials have been chosen for durability.

Tables in this book are reprinted
with permission from the Victoria Advocate.

Library of Congress Cataloging-in-Publication Data

Quiroz, Anthony, 1958–
Claiming citizenship : Mexican Americans in Victoria, Texas / Anthony Quiroz
    p. cm. — (Fronteras series ; no. 3)
Includes bibliographical references and index.
1.Mexican Americans—Texas—Victoria—Politics and government.
2.Victoria (Tex.)—Ethnic relations—Political aspects. I. Title. II. Series.
F394.V6Q57 2005
323.1168720730764125—dc22
2004015209

ISBN 13: 978-1-58544-410-6 (cloth)
ISBN 13: 978-1-60344-986-1 (paper)
ISBN 13: 978-1-60344-591-7 (ebook)

To Pat, Lisa, Eric, and Steven

Contents

Preface   ix
Introduction   xv

Chapter 1
From Mexican Colony to Anglo Stronghold:
An Overview of Two Centuries of
Victoria's History   3

Chapter 2
"For God, for Country, for Home":
The Catholic Church and Mexican American
Identity Formation   24

Chapter 3
Creating Loyal Citizens:
The Relationship between Mexican Americans
and the Victoria Independent School District   49

Chapter 4
"By the Power of Reason":
The Role of Community-Based Mexican American
Organizations on Identity Formation, 1940–85   77

Chapter 5
Strength through Adversity:
Struggles for Political Inclusion   99

Conclusion   125
Notes   129
Bibliography   147
Index   159

Preface

O N A warm autumn day in 1968 two friends, one white, one Mexican American, were talking in the lunch line at a Catholic grammar school. The Anglo child, the son of a prominent local banker, had been talking about his family's summer getaway on a lake where they swam, fished, hiked, and generally had a wonderful time. "Why don't you come with us one weekend?" he asked his young buddy. The Mexican American child thought that such a weekend sounded like a lot of fun and agreed to ask his parents' permission. Happy that their son was in Catholic school and hoping that he would grow up to be a respected professional someday, the young boy's parents readily agreed to let him go with his friend some weekend. A day or so later the two boys were again talking and the Mexican American boy asked his Anglo friend about the weekend getaway. "Oh, I'm sorry but you can't go. Daddy said he didn't want no niggers at our place." Initially confused by such a response, the Mexican American boy pushed further, "But I'm not . . ." "I know," replied the white child, "and I told him, 'But Daddy, he ain't a nigger, he's a meskin,'" to which his father simply repeated the earlier statement and ended the conversation.

I relate this story because I was the Mexican American boy in that story. After that incident, my friend and I drifted apart. We remained on good terms, but it was clear that our worlds were not meant to meet. This was only one in a string of incidents in which I was continually reminded of who I was and how I fit into the social order. Attending an overwhelmingly Anglo Catholic school, my friends were Anglo. The white middle class informed the public arena in which I participated. My language was English. My culture became American popular culture. At their homes, even their parents and siblings would remark about bad "meskins" in front of me, all the time assuring me, "It's okay, we don't mean you. You're a good meskin." At the time, these remarks were confusing but easily forgettable. Racism is a curious thing. It has a way of subtly inhering itself on the landscape so that after a point it appears normal. I was pleasantly surprised when attending graduate school in Iowa at the ways in which my new friends shuddered at the mention of such racial epithets. For many Texans such terms as "nigger" and "meskin" or "greaser" were just a part of the accepted vernacular growing up: "There's a tree, there's a car, there's a meskin." Just a statement of fact. And so it was for those two little boys trying subconsciously to build bridges in 1968. They were simply two friends looking for companionship. The world quickly set them straight. No bridges were to be built that year.

The nature of the conversation between my friend and his father about me was telling in ways that I did not fully appreciate at the time. For his father, nonwhites could be categorized together with a single epithet. Certainly he understood the visible differences between an African American and a Mexican American, but to him those differences did not matter. It was the difference between white and nonwhite that defined "acceptable" and "nonacceptable" citizens, and noncitizens. His son's clear differentiation between the two groups, while unfortunate in terms of language choice, indicated that he accepted a more multilayered understanding of race and, although he would likely not have used the term at the time, "citizenship" as well.

My experience growing up in Victoria was in some ways exemplary. Surrounded by a culture that emphasized assimilation and the superiority of white middle-class values and culture while denigrating my Mexican past, I learned to adapt and assimilate. Through the years, however, I learned that assimilation was meant to be a one-way street. I was to learn English properly, abandon Spanish completely, and accept the ideals of the social studies curriculum, which centered on a belief in the superiority of American (i.e., white) political traditions, economic systems, and social structures: the stuff of "citizens." I was, in other words, expected to internalize the values, practices, traits, and beliefs that anchored the ideology of citizenship. Acceptance of such precepts, so I was taught, would prepare me for success in an increasingly color-blind society. What I did not realize at the time was that these touchstone beliefs had been claimed as the creation of white society. Nonwhites had to learn to accept them in order to become welcomed into Americanhood.

Instances such as that with my friend in fourth grade were compounded over time as I found out that white society simply wanted me, and others like me, to acquiesce and not to question, to be satisfied with a marginal existence. The true goal of assimilation was not to equip Mexican American students with the skills necessary to compete for prominent leadership positions within the city. Rather, it was to teach minority students to be patriotic and accept civic responsibilities but to not challenge their designated place in that society. Hence we could eat in the same school cafeteria with the children of white elites, or even play on the same sports teams, but we could neither marry their children, nor could we expect lucrative job offers to join their law firms or banks.

Generally speaking, society's objective of creating proper Americans among Victoria's minority population seems to have worked. That is my impression, as Victoria, Texas, is the town in which I was raised. The story that follows is typical of the lives of Mexican Americans throughout the U.S. Southwest, yet is one that appears on the surface to be atypical because of the seemingly anomalous reactions of Victoria's Mexican Americans to their circumstances. Theirs is not a chronicle of overt resistance, labor organization, strikes, demonstrations, or riots. Neither does their story echo themes that involved rejection of capitalism or democracy, or republicanism, or even Anglo culture and society.

Victoria's Mexican Americans did engage in struggles for equal citizenship throughout the twentieth century, but they consistently did so as the loyal opposition. As such, they opposed the exclusionary social, cultural, political, and economic status quo founded on the notion of white supremacy by employing the tools of citizenry: the courts, the vote, and education. Various individuals and groups, beginning in the 1940s, worked to bring about integrated schools, better political representation, and quality education. They also sought to create a professional class of Mexican Americans whose public respectability would help advance the cause of Mexican equality. Just as a rising tide lifts all boats, Mexican American doctors, lawyers, accountants, teachers, and engineers, it was believed, would constitute a critical mass of intelligent, educated leaders who could uplift the well-being of the entire Mexican community. But an ill-defined, nonarticulated, and widely understood and accepted set of values, practices, traits, and beliefs muted the potential for radicalism. The quest for public legitimacy was thus undertaken within the framework of a bicultural identity that was adaptable to the private Mexican world of home, church, neighborhood, and family, as well as the public world of school, work, and politics. Coexistence with Anglo-American society and a partaking of the American dream was the desired ideal.

Completion of this work has been my dream for numerous years, dating back to the mid-1990s when it was still in the early dissertation stage. I have successfully attained this dream because of the help of numerous individuals and groups. I would thus like to thank the people in the history department at the University of Iowa, in particular my advisor Shel Stromquist. Shel's constant reassurance as I wrote the dissertation while working full time at Texas A&M–Corpus Christi sustained me through two years of incredibly long days of teaching, committee work, and writing. Further, Alan Steinberg and Leslie Schwalm were supportive throughout the dissertation phase and beyond.

Numerous people at various institutions offered invaluable assistance with the research. I would thus like to thank the personnel at the library of the Texas Educational Agency, the Catholic Archives, the Nettie Lee Benson Latin American Collection of the University of Texas, and the Texas State Archives, all in Austin. Additionally, the staff at the Victoria Public Library and the library of the Victoria College/University of Houston–Victoria as well as the Archives of the Archdioceses of San Antonio and Victoria, Texas, were instrumental in my research. I would also like to thank Gloria Espitia of University of Houston-Victoria for all her hard work in helping me attain the photographs for this work. Dr. Thomas H. Kreneck and his assistants (Grace Charles in particular) in the Special Collections and Archives of Bell Library at Texas A&M–Corpus Christi made reading through the mammoth Dr. Hector P. García papers a manageable and enjoyable experience.

Entering my first job ABD (all but dissertation) was quite a daunting challenge. Without the help and understanding of the fine folks on the faculty and staff of the College of Arts and Humanities this project would not have been completed. Hence, I appreciate deeply the support of my colleagues at Texas A&M–Corpus Christi, particularly Pat Carroll, Robert Wooster, and Alan Lessoff. Their belief in me sometimes outweighed my own, and gave me the courage to see this project through to the end.

I was allowed valuable free time to work on the manuscript, turning it from a verbose dissertation to a sharply focused book only with the help of an Extending the Reach: Faculty Research Award from the National Endowment for the Humanities, an independent federal agency. Without such assistance this book would have been several additional years in the making.

Numerous individuals offered useful commentary on various portions of the work through conference presentations or in personal conversations. Thank you Rudy Rocha, Dionício Valdes, Myrna Santiago.

I would like to offer special thanks to Arnoldo De León whom I have come to view as a mentor and friend. His exacting standards and sharp criticisms of earlier drafts of this book forced me to think through my arguments and improve dramatically my ability to articulate those ideas. His patience and inspiration carried me through moments of self-doubt, helped me think that maybe I was on to something, and gave me the confidence to finish.

A version of chapter 4 previously appeared as "Mexican American Struggles for Citizenship: Local Organizations in Twentieth Century, Victoria, Texas" in *South Texas Studies* 7 (1996). A more theoretical version of chapter 4 previously appeared as "Claiming Citizenship: Class and Consensus in a Mexican American Community" in the *Southwestern Historical Quarterly* 106 (July 1, 2002).

A version of chapter 1 was published under the title "Carving out a Place of Their Own: Mexican American Catholics in Victoria, Texas" in the *Catholic Southwest* 14 (Summer 2003): 11–27.

Introduction

CARLOS SOLÍS was born in Saltillo in the Mexican state of Coahuila on November 4, 1903. He immigrated to the United States in June, 1926, working in San Antonio until September when he moved to Victoria where he found employment as a carpenter. Solís never joined a union. He never picketed a business or government institution. He was never arrested or attacked by the police. Yet neither was he satisfied with the state of relations between Mexican Americans and Anglo-Americans he found in Victoria in the 1920s. Solís, therefore, became an activist for social change, seeking to create a more egalitarian world for his family. But in that activism Solís never challenged the core structure of American society. Indeed, he accepted the existent economic and political systems in principle. His concerns lay with the marginalization and discrimination that Mexican Americans like himself experienced.[1]

Victoria's other Mexican American activists after World War II, like Solís, also questioned the inequities of American society while simultaneously embracing its structure and the spoken and unspoken values, practices, traits, and beliefs that had come to define first-class American citizenship. World War II, according to most scholars, was a watershed event in the history of Mexican American identity formation. Returning veterans, their families, and friends saw Mexican American war involvement at home and abroad as evidence of their community's patriotism. Their contributions to the war and the experiences gained from it emboldened Mexican Americans to challenge a racist social order that had traditionally cast them as second-class citizens. Negotiating primarily through the classroom, the ballot box, and the court (only in rare instances did activists engage in strikes or demonstrations), Victoria's Mexican Americans during and after World War II actively and aggressively challenged the predominant, narrow definitions of American citizenship created and guarded by the Anglo majority.

The World War II victory over fascism and the emerging cold war against communism signified a dramatic change in the primary markers of citizenship. More clearly than before citizenship in the cold war years came to be defined in ideological terms by mainstream society. This is not to suggest that racialized concepts of citizenship disappeared. Quite the contrary, the new ideological struggle against communism gave racists a new language and new rhetorical weaponry, which they marshaled against the rising tide of civil rights sentiment. Support for equal status in the early cold war years could be undermined by linking it with that supposed worst of all evils — communism.

Ironically, the increased desires for social justice embraced by the civil rights movement stemmed in part from the new anticommunist understanding of citizenship, for postwar emphasis on ideological conformity seemed to offer access to citizenship for those who were willing to embrace certain ideological prescripts that stood as antithetical to the temptations of fascism or communism. Mass culture, individualism, and consumerism, and the mythology of American exceptionalism at midcentury, further shaped new notions of rights owed to those living in the era. Such understandings engendered fertile intellectual ground for Mexican Americans to question long-standing exclusionary definitions of citizenship in two ways. First, as legal loyal citizens, Mexican Americans could now make claims on society for public legitimacy. If the United States was to convincingly promote itself globally as the superior alternative to communism, it had to emphasize not only its economic but also its political and social superiority. The egalitarianism embedded within the American language of politics opened the door for Mexican Americans to challenge exclusionary political and legal definitions of citizenship. In confronting the status quo, Mexican Americans never sought a dramatic cultural shift of any sort, rather, they hoped to maintain their language, customs, and traditions, and legitimize them by showing that these characteristics could exist in ideological harmony with the antiradical mentality advocated by mainstream (white) culture. This desire to join a unified American effort that would stand against socialism allowed for a second challenge to discrimination. If Mexican Americans could prove that they had internalized specific ideas, they could call for a renegotiation of definitions of citizenship, which, at least in the public discourse, were increasingly, though never completely, driven by ideology.

CONSENSUS CONSTITUTED the major feature of the cold war thinking prevalent within Mexican American society in Texas, and by extension, Victoria. At least five considerations defined this generally accepted worldview. The first, an identity as American, is traceable to the 1920s, as evidenced by the formation of organizations such as Order of Sons of America, formed in 1921, and the League of United Latin American Citizens (LULAC), formed in 1929. Not exclusively, but increasingly, segments of the Victoria community after World War I (1914–19) were also beginning to see themselves as Americans who happened to be Mexican, more so than as Mexicans who happened to live in America.[2] With such incipient identity formation, the nature of Mexican American resistance to Anglo domination experienced a dramatic change as LULAC by the 1930s was challenging old definitions of citizenship through the courts and various other frameworks. This would be the kind of resistance in which Mexican Americans in Victoria engaged throughout the post–World War II years, including the years of the Chicano movement (1966–75) and beyond.

The acceptance of what were widely considered to be fundamental norms was a second force contributing to the manner in which post–World War II Mexican Americans would approach their struggle for equal citizenship. Mexican Americans accepted what were perceived to be American values such as materialism, Christianity, family, patriotism, and the work ethic. They also embraced other aspects of American core values: practices such as political participation; traits of character such as dependability and responsibility; beliefs such as the superiority of capitalism, and conversely, the dangers of fascism, socialism, or any other perceived type of extremism; and the loftiness of what historians have identified as the dominant middle-class culture. Even though many of these prerequisites were already a part of Mexican culture (family, Christianity, work ethic among many others), they were marked in the popular Anglo mind as the creation and proprietorship of white America.

Apparent agreement among social classes over the definitions of citizenship constituted a third factor shaping the post–World War II approach to equality in Victoria. Ingrained American beliefs cut across class lines within the Mexican American community. Class affected Victoria's Mexican Americans, but in less profound ways than current theoretical assumptions presume. Victoria's Mexican Americans experienced class-awareness, but never developed a strong sense of it, nor did they develop widely divergent goals and strategies because of that difference. And while there were tensions between the middle and working classes on personal levels, overall the groups and individuals from each group maintained a similar ideology that was based on a shared sense of oppression and destiny. Culturally, the Mexican American community wished to maintain the Spanish language and Mexican traditions. But socially, economically, and politically, there were strong desires to accept, not the social status quo, but the fundamental premises of society that these individuals believed held the ideological promise and offered the rationale to bring to an end, or at least challenge seriously, a long-standing tradition of discrimination informed by exclusionary definitions of citizenship.

The widespread acceptance of a mainstream ideology that contributed to the absence of class-consciousness caused Victoria's Mexican Americans to narrowly and carefully define the parameters of acceptable types of dissent. This mindset muted a priori almost any prospects of "radicalism" within the community. For Victoria's Mexican Americans, the only permissible avenues for protest involved options such as the ballot box and the lawsuit to gain acceptance as equal citizens.[3] The years from 1945 to the present are filled with examples of Mexican Americans working (as individuals and in organizations) to increase political participation and suing businesses and governmental entities, citing Constitutional protection as equal citizens, to challenge discriminatory practices.

The last determinant of Victoria's cold war civic activism was the Mexican American belief that education held the key to economic success, public respectability, and political power. Education was understood as requisite to creating a visible, viable, and professional cadre. Through the growth of a professional wing of the Mexican American middle class, Mexican Americans promoted themselves as equal citizens interested in the welfare of the general society as well as their own upward mobility. Professionalism, it was widely believed, carried the status required to acquire the public validation necessary to assert influence. Mexican Americans in Victoria believed that the attainment of middle class status through education validated their challenges to the existing racist order.

A predominant consensus thus pervaded the political mood in Victoria during the last half of the twentieth century. This frame of mind limited the range of acceptable avenues for protest thereby discouraging overt challenges to Anglo domination. In the context of Mexican American history elsewhere, Victoria's Mexican Americans appear to be a people for whom, "it seemed like nothing happened."[4]

One significant reason why Victoria's history appears so inert is that in many ways it stands in stark contrast to the historical literature that focuses heavily on Mexican American resistance and confrontation with Anglo society. Action that appears to be cooperative or consensual, as was the case in Victoria, is rarely dealt with at length. Moreover, traditional scholarship stresses the victimization of Mexican Americans. My work, by contrast, focuses on attempted conformity, coexistence, and collaboration, especially as practiced by the articulate portion of the Mexican American community.[5]

One example of the literature that stands in stark contrast to this work is Armando Navarro's *The Cristal Experiment: A Chicano Struggle for Community Control.*[6] Navarro tells the tale of a people who were "politically apathetic and abased," but who, in reaction to an "exogenous precondition" (the civil rights movement) and "endogenous preconditions" arising from local controversies coupled with "rising expectations of Mexicanos,"[7] experienced a political awakening and a change in consciousness in the late 1950s and into the 1960s. But at the heart of the movement in *Cristal* was a cadre of activists, particularly José Angel Gutiérrez, who acted as crystallizing agents and brought virtually the entire community together under a cohesive ideology of protest.

Victoria lacked the unifying force of prominent figures such as José Angel Gutiérrez (Texas), César Chávez (California), Reies López Tijerina (New Mexico), or Rodolfo "Corky" Gonzáles (Colorado). Instead, various local groups and individuals emerged as leaders in one front or another at different times, and rarely in harmony with other activists. Indeed, the two most significant civil rights organizations in the city experienced internal splits themselves as will be explained in chapter 4. The absence of a consistently powerful single leader or organization, with an attendant consensual ideological framework, meant that Victoria's Mexican Americans took a more pragmatic, nonideological approach to reform.

In telling this very different story about Victoria, I have been strongly influenced by Alex Saragoza's call for new directions in Chicano history. Saragoza contends that the traditional "them-versus-us" model (and the undergirding theme of victimization) holds limited explanatory power.[8] This is not to argue that there was no conflict in Victoria. Indeed, the evidence bears out a story of antagonism that continues to the present. The problem with the "us versus them" model is that the themes of victimization and conflict tend to draw scholars to stories that support specific assumptions and create a monolithic image of social groups such as Mexican Americans and Anglos. The homogenizing effects of this emphasis on a singular collective history obscure important distinctions of experience among the Mexican American communities across the United States. Compared to people in other towns in Texas, for instance, Victoria's Mexican Americans never forged a strong sense of class-consciousness, nor did identifiable segments of the Mexican American community develop distinct goals and strategies because of class differences. Thus, there emerged in Victoria a consensual worldview that had a unifying effect across class lines and allowed for a sense of ideological cohesion centered on patriotism and anti-radicalism that paralleled mainstream values.

Another problem with the "us versus them" model is the way in which it has tended to homogenize the experiences and worldviews of Mexican Americans. The work of Mario T. García has, perhaps, gone the furthest to create a more heterogeneous image of Mexican American history.[9] His work on the creation of a bicultural Mexican identity in El Paso and his examination of the Mexican American generation and its political ideology have advanced our understanding of the ways in which Mexican Americans have struggled against discrimination. Yet even in García's *Mexican Americans* we see a traditional, class-based analysis of differences within the Mexican American community. Hence, García's middle class is dedicated to political action and education, and his working class is focused on leftist-inspired labor organizing. In Victoria, by contrast, workers and the middle class were interested in education and political activism, and neither appears to have been inspired by leftist ideology in any form.

THIS BOOK is not meant to be a comprehensive history of twentieth-century Victoria. It is, instead, an attempted overview of the twentieth-century Mexican American experience in the city with a strong focus primarily on the post–World War II years. It was during the 1940s and after that the most dramatic changes listed above occurred. While Mexican Americans in Victoria, for the most part, never completely surrendered their language and culture, they did after World War II increasingly embrace the ideological aspects of Americanism that they felt would open the door to political and economic incorporation. Rather than seeing such a choice as a compromise of their identity, Hispanic Victorians saw this move as a clear, and substantive step toward dealing with the racist status quo. By creating an Americanized professional class, and thereby gaining access to improved living conditions and upward mobility, Mexican Americans in Victoria could lay claim to public legitimacy and call themselves American citizens. This very process changed the meaning of the earlier definition of "American." If American citizenship had been defined as much by negatives (who was not an American), as by positives (who was), then acculturation changed not only what it meant to be an ethnic Mexican living in the United States but also the meaning of what it was to be American at all.

This emphasis on participants and how they pursued social action leads to a necessary discussion of ethnic labels. In the portions of the book that focus on the nineteenth century, the word "Mexican" refers to ethnic Mexicans during the early nineteenth century, regardless of place of birth. Once Texas achieved independence, two words emerged to describe non-Indian inhabitants: Texian in reference to whites, and Tejano in reference to Mexicans residing in Texas. Thus, portions of the work that address ethnic Mexicans during the period 1836 to 1900 will employ the word Tejano. Around the turn of the century, however, continued immigration from Mexico meant that people of Mexican descent living in Texas were largely foreign born, and so the term Mexicano is more appropriate. After World War I, however, Mexicans living in the United States increasingly began to articulate an identity as American citizens of Mexican descent. From that point forward, therefore, the phrase Mexican American becomes more appropriate and historically accurate. The Chicano movement of the 1960s and 1970s had minimal impact in Victoria, but there too, when young militant activists are mentioned in chapter 5, they are discussed as Chicanos. Hence, in this work, the terms Mexican, Mexicano, Tejano, Mexican American, and Chicano will be neither synonymous nor interchangeable, although they do refer to members of the same ethnic group. Such a complicated method of description is necessary in order to remain true to the perspectives of the historical actors under study. Only in the last chapters will the terms Hispanic and Mexican American be used synonymously as those terms have evolved, in recent years, to be roughly equivalent in the region.

For the purposes of this work, "white" will refer not only to a racial group but also to the ideology, lifestyle, and status, which, in the Anglo public consciousness, were deemed to be the product of Western European Protestant capitalist culture. This racialized American Weltanschauung unfolded gradually throughout the eighteenth and nineteenth centuries and imposed itself over American political and public culture. Hence, one significant step many groups have historically taken in order to gain equal citizenship has been to embrace the values deemed by mainstream culture as normative and which were widely considered to be products of Anglo-American culture and Western European traditions. In this way, some groups such as the Irish and Italians became generally accepted as part of the mainstream. They achieved whiteness, and with it—the public's trust. For the Irish and Italians, the movement from "other" to "citizen" was eased by virtue of their skin color.[10] Even though "whiteness" in this work is meant to imply an ideological construct rather than a racial one, color remained a part of what shaped people's perceptions of who qualified to be granted full citizenship and who did not.

Mexican Americans, unlike European immigrant groups, however, were less willing to embrace an Anglo-American identity. Mexican Americans in Victoria worked to attain the requisite levels of economic, educational, and political status to be considered equals deserving of full citizenship. In so doing, they focused on ideas and actions, making only limited cultural and social concessions. The result was a people who accepted the essential structure of society while challenging, through "acceptable" channels, existent inequalities based on ethnicity. Discussing the Mexican American political activists involved in the 1960 election, historian Ignacio García finds a similar ideology: "They challenged discrimination at all levels, yet they remained optimistic that American society was fundamentally fair." [11] Victoria's Mexican Americans sustained a parallel view.

This story of consensual opposition will be told in two parts. The first consists of one chapter that provides a chronological overview of Victoria's founding and growth. The final four chapters examine various areas of Mexican American activism. Because of the consistency of a consensual worldview within Victoria's Mexican American community, it is difficult to periodize effectively the history of Mexican Americans in Victoria. And since Victoria's Mexican Americans never developed a singular all-encompassing movement, but instead featured groups and individuals with essentially similar goals and roughly similar strategies and tactics, some chapters are organized chronologically while others are organized topically, telling the stories of various groups whose stories overlap chronologically.

Hence, chapter 1 gives a brief overview of nineteenth- and twentieth-century Victoria history, showing how Victoria was transformed from a Mexican colony in 1824 to a town dominated by whites immediately after the Texas revolution of 1836. During that era, whites in Victoria organized the town along racial and economic lines in ways that effectively marginalized Tejanos. The second half of the chapter offers an overview of the shaping of the south side barrio as it responded to changes in Victoria during the first half of the twentieth century. As the city grew to the north and west and as the economy diversified and flourished, discrimination limited, although it did not eliminate, Mexican Americans' abilities to participate fully in Victoria's ripening prosperity. Simultaneously, the chapter looks into the Americanization that occurred among Mexican Americans in the city's south side and why they began fashioning their own definition of citizenship. Together both halves of the chapter help establish a context for the oppressive environment Mexican Americans faced in the second half of the twentieth century: one that anchored citizenship on a concept of normative behavior identifiable with the white race, and that stigmatized Mexicans as "other" and therefore not equal as citizens or human beings. It was this legacy that incited post–World War II activism, as detailed in chapters 2 through 5.

Chapter 2 examines the ways in which the Catholic Church throughout the century acted to promote (and at times inhibit) the inclusion of Mexican Americans into Victorian society. Throughout the century, Mexican Americans faced anti-Catholic bias and religious bigotry, but Catholicism gradually gained acceptance into the parameters of normative. As that occurred the Catholic Church in Victoria became at once the site for desires to maintain Mexican culture and for the expression of a broad consensual vision of citizenship.

The third chapter analyzes the ways in which the public school system was originally designed as a tool for segregation and a conduit for the maintenance of the status quo. The chapter demonstrates how the relationship between the Mexican American community and the public schools became an arena in which the assigned social roles for Mexican Americans were contested. By closing the separate Mexican school in 1917, and later in the 1970s and 1980s by mounting challenges to discriminatory hiring practices and curricula, Mexican Americans used the issue of education as a vehicle for the expression of their desires for equal citizenship. Education was widely seen as the single most valuable avenue for gaining equality. Through education, so activists believed, Mexican American youth could become part of the professional elite and attain the economic power and social prestige necessary for changing the definition of American citizenship.

Chapter 4 focuses on the role Mexican American organizations — local, state, and national — played in shaping identity and assisting in the struggle for citizenship. These organizations exhibited the varied viewpoints and experiences informing the Mexican American community in the period under study, as well as an overwhelming consensus that caused different groups to express similar visions for change. This discussion shows a cross-class consensus driven by acceptance of a set of beliefs, values, and behaviors that moderated tendencies toward class-consciousness.

The fifth and final chapter focuses on political developments in the city and chronicles Mexican American struggles for political enfranchisement after World War II. Due to the activities of various community and civic organizations, the assistance of civil rights legislation, and a growing middle class, Mexican Americans moved closer during this era toward equal political participation and representation. This chapter describes the ways in which Mexican Americans worked within the system they accepted in an effort to bring about evolutionary change. The virtual lack of militance or direct confrontation indicated not a passive acquiescence but rather desires to marshal the ammunition of citizenship (the ballot box and the courts) to gain deserved political equality.[12]

These chapters together show how Victoria's Mexican Americans followed a different path (compared to other communities) to equality, a path of their own choosing. Their historical experiences and actions provide another way of understanding twentieth-century Mexican American history by challenging commonly held historiographical assumptions in two ways. First, they contribute to a more complex image of the Mexican American historical experience than currently exists. Whether consciously or not, the extant literature tends to create a rather bifurcated past in which workers organized and fought injustice at the workplace (be it the migrant farmworkers' fields or the shop floor) while the middle class sought to protect its narrow interests or promoted gradual social improvement through accommodation. The presence and importance of Chicanismo has been examined in detail from the farm fields of California, to Denver, to the political expression of the Raza Unida Party. The proliferation of studies of such actions implies an almost universality about *el movimiento*. Events in Victoria challenge both notions. In Victoria there was a virtual total absence of class-consciousness. Indeed, one finds example after example of behaviors that contradict current assumptions based on class analyses. The Chicano movement almost missed Victoria. Certainly there was a mild movement in the city, but it was brief, weakly supported, and generally ineffectual. While perhaps no single author has attempted to argue that Chicanismo was a universal experience, the direction of Chicano-movement literature lends itself to that conclusion. The seemingly atypical behavior of Victoria's Mexican Americans leads to the second way in which their story contradicts current historiographical implications. The historical experiences and actions of people in Victoria redefine ideas of accommodation and resistance. Certainly this book acts to muddle the distinction between the two, but this blurring enriches and de-homogenizes our understanding of what it has historically meant to be Mexican American. In this book I argue that the presence of conflict and resistance designed to beget social change over time existed in Victoria, but did not override consensualism apropos to citizenship and the manner to achieve equal status.

Claiming Citizenship

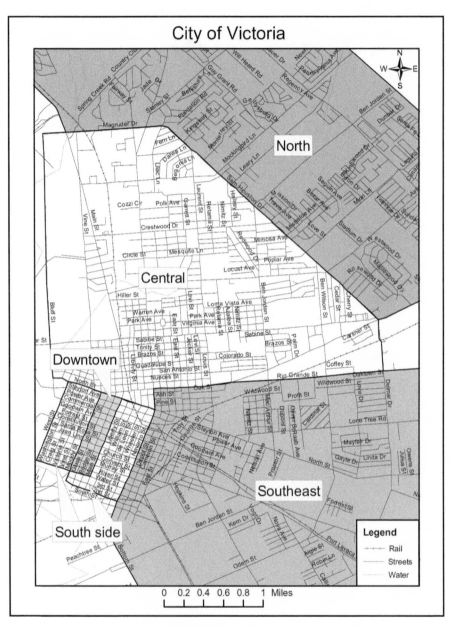

City of Victoria. *Map produced by Rick Smith, Texas A&M–Corpus Christi*

From Mexican Colony to Anglo Stronghold

An Overview of Two Centuries

of Victoria's History

VICTORIA began as a small *empresario* community along the banks of the Guadalupe River in 1824. The subsequent twelve years marked a brief period of relative racial harmony in the colony comprised of a majority of Mexican families and a minority of Irish settlers. But in the immediate aftermath of the Texas Revolution Anglo Texans dismantled the old social structure and replaced it with a new order that was founded upon white supremacy. From that point forward, Anglos imposed on the community a definition of "citizen" that in their ethos excluded nonwhites. The new construction of citizenship required the acceptance of certain values that Texians claimed as unique to themselves. In this restructuring, Anglos controlled the nascent political, economic, and social systems, which relegated Tejanos to a subordinate condition. Because of the limitations of this post-1836 arrangement, Tejanos were effectively marginalized from equal participation in Anglo-dominant society.

This pattern of oppression continued into the twentieth century. As the city industrialized and grew in population, the old Anglo-dominant social restrictions continued unabated. Even the experience of combating the racist regime of the Nazis in World War II and a national fear of communist subversion were not powerful enough centripetal forces to overcome a longstanding tradition of racism against Mexican Americans.

The rest of this chapter stands in two parts. The first will detail the ways in which Victoria moved from a small, quiet, peaceful Mexican *pueblo* to a community that was hostile and sometimes violent toward Tejanos and that created the circumstances against which Mexican Americans had to struggle for equality later in the twentieth century. The second will present an overview of Victoria's geographic and economic history in the twentieth century while chronicling the continuance of racist practices. In its entirety this chapter paints a picture of the social environment in which Mexican Americans struggled for equality.

MARTÍN DE LEÓN, the founder of Victoria, was an adventuresome, ambitious gentleman. Born in Burgos, Mexico, in 1765, at the age of twenty he joined the Fieles de Burgos, a militia company created by the government of New Spain to combat Indian incursions. While traversing South Texas on business in 1805, de León passed through the area where he would found Victoria. He was impressed with the region's multitude of deer and wild horses, abundant water from the Guadalupe River, large supply of timber, and arable soil. In addition to its natural resources, the future Victoria area was also situated on the main route from Mexico City to New Orleans and was the site of the first low-water crossing on the Guadalupe River.[1] De León consequently petitioned for an empresario contract to settle on his newly explored land. Although the Mexican government rejected de León's initial request for colonization, he persisted and in April of 1824 the Provincial Deputation approved his petition for a colonization contract. In the course of reviewing de León's application, Mexican officials, in an attempt to honor President Guadalupe Victoria, added the name "Victoria" to the grant's name. It became Villa de Nuestra Señora de Guadalupe Victoria Nombre de Jesús.[2]

De León's contract required him to settle forty families but due to unexpected economic problems only twelve of those families accompanied him in 1824 on the northward trek to establish his colony. But he found eight Irish families already living within the boundaries of his grant upon his arrival. Rather than evicting them, he allowed the Europeans to remain. Among the Irish pioneers were John J. Linn, John D. Wright, and Joseph Ware, all of whom played important roles later in the development of the community.[3] By 1829 de León's colony numbered thirty-three Mexican families and eight white families, thus surpassing by one the original goal of forty families.[4]

From 1824 to 1836 Mexican-Irish relations in Victoria remained cordial. Indeed, John Linn, one of the founding Irish settlers, became a prominent figure in the nascent colony. Linn was elected *alcalde* of Victoria in 1836 and presently a major downtown thoroughfare bears the name "Juan Linn." The friendly coexistence between the two original groups of settlers in the Victoria area can be explained in part by the fact that Irish immigrants did not bring the kind of malevolent, Anglocentric ideology that some Americans imported to Texas.

The successful Centralist Party takeover of power in Mexico in 1834 led to resistance in many parts of the country including Texas and its fledgling community of Guadalupe Victoria where residents, both Mexican and Irish, swore their allegiance to the Mexican Constitution of 1824.[5] Mexicans from Victoria actively opposed Antonio López de Santa Anna and his Centralist forces by serving as militia leaders and on committees of correspondence. Silvestre de León, Fernando de León, John McHenry, and John J. Linn organized the town's citizenry in opposition to the Mexican dictator.[6] When it became clear that reinstatement of the 1824 Constitution was not likely, Victorians supported the Texas independence movement.[7] Santa Anna subsequently ordered the arrest of José M. Carbajal of Victoria for treason. When the military went to arrest him, Plácido Benavides, alcalde and son-in-law of Martín de León (by now deceased), met the Mexican detachment sent to arrest Carbajal and informed the soldiers that the city would not turn Carbajal over to Centralist authorities.[8] During the revolution Benavides along with Silvestre de León and other members of the family led a company of thirty Mexican ranchers who helped bring about the surrender of General Martín Perfecto de Cós in San Antonio in December, 1835. When in 1836, after securing the fort at La Bahía, General José Urrea took Victoria, he immediately arrested Fernando de León.[9]

Unfortunately for Fernando de León, the Mexican military forced him to expose a cache of arms outside the city that was intended for resistance against the Centralists. This act was later interpreted by Anglos as treasonous and used as grounds for confiscation of de León's land. Thus did the once-great de León family, founders of the city of Guadalupe Victoria, find themselves persona non grata in their own homeland. The animosity exhibited toward the de León family displayed latent patterns of bigotry and mistrust among the new ruling circle that consisted of U.S. immigrants. As one historian put it, "Almost immediately," following the battle of San Jacinto, "Victoria was completely changed from a quiet Mexican town to a wild Anglo-American town, dominated by an army and many newcomers that distrusted and hated the Mexicans."[10] The newly ascended Anglo majority now defined citizenship according to its own prescriptions. From this point forward, Victoria's Mexicans became second-class residents.

Many of them, including the de León family, faced land displacement. On June 19, 1836, General Thomas Rusk ordered "Families Mexicans and all to fall back at once and clear the County." A subsequent "special order" called for certain people in the Victoria area to "remove east instantly." Hence, despite the de Leóns' support of the revolutionary cause against Santa Anna, and their decision to seek complete Texas independence, the Victorians were forced to flee to Opelousas, Louisiana, where they had business contacts.[11] Rusk personally sent men to escort the de León and Carbajal families out of town and see to it that they boarded vessels bound for Louisiana.[12] As the early de León family chronicler A. B. J. Hammett put it:

> This family like other loyal Mexican families were driven from their homes, their treasures, their cattle and horses and their lands, by an army of reckless, war-crazy people, who overran the town of Victoria. These new people distrusted and hated the Mexicans, simply because they were Mexican, regardless of the fact they were both on the same side of the fighting during the war.[13]

Not all Mexicans, however, suffered economic ruin or saw expulsion.[14] Of the fifty-two Tejano families that either remained in Victoria County during the revolution or left and returned, only ten had to sue in order to maintain their land, and of these, eight succeeded. In fact, when land taxes were reimposed by President Sam Houston in 1844 and 1845 none of the fifty-two sheriff's sales in the county involved a Mexican landowner.[15] Anglo ranchers too, such as James Power, found their claims challenged by unscrupulous, ambitious newcomers who took advantage of changes in property laws to challenge the rights of previous landowners.[16]

Recent scholarship has pointed to reasons other than Anglo machinations as possible causes of Mexican land loss. Ana Carolina Castillo Crimm attributes the decline of Mexican property holdings, and coincidentally Mexican power and influence, to partible inheritance practices.[17]

> [L]and-holding Mexican-American families faced the difficult choices of how to leave land to their heirs. To share the land equally was to destroy the very wealth which had permitted the Mexican-Americans to live comfortably in the Anglo society. The Anglo-American custom of primogeniture left all but one of the heirs with no legacy at all. For the Mexican Americans, the equal division of the land was a necessity. As generation followed generation the land was divided into smaller and smaller portions and the heirs faced a choice of trying to make a living on the smaller parcels or to move to other areas. Some did remain but other Mexican Americans from Victoria migrated to the cities or to other parts of Texas, where they joined Germans, Anglo-Americans and freed southern blacks in locating new farms and ranches.[18]

According to Crimm, it was the tradition of dividing one's land among heirs rather than legal chicanery and forcible displacement that undermined Mexican landownership in Victoria. While Crimm indeed makes a compelling case that in many instances Mexican landowners, however unwittingly, undermined their own success, it must also be remembered that whatever land dislocation Tejanos suffered in Victoria occurred in a hostile social environment.

In fact, the 1840s and 1850s were a period of increased antipathy toward Mexicans both in Victoria and around Texas. The actions of Santa Anna's army dovetailed with Anglo assumptions about cruelty inherent in the "Black Legend," and thus were associated in the popular Anglo mind with the bloodthirsty nature of Mexicans. For many Texians before the Civil War, the battle cry "Remember the Alamo" carried a racial weight that indicated a belief that the Texas Revolution was really a struggle between the forces of Anglo-American values and traditions and backward, "savage" Mexicans.[19]

An episode in 1842 further deepened Anglo views of the barbaric nature of Mexicans. In response to the two Mexican invasions of Texas that year, President Sam Houston ordered Alexander Somervell and 750 volunteers to Laredo; the subsequent events produced the ill-fated Mier expedition. Of the original force that accompanied Somervell, fifty were from Victoria. Of the 300 involved in the attack on Mier, thirty-four hailed from Victoria. Of those captured, twenty-eight took part in the "black bean incident," resulting in four of their deaths. The Mexican army later shot a fifth volunteer on special orders of Santa Anna.[20]

Such actions fed the already vile view that Anglos had of Mexicans and gave Anglo Victorians more reasons to view Mexicans negatively as "other." In short order, Mexicans became barbarous, innately inferior, and impediments to progress. Because Anglos set the terms of public discourse, the word "Mexican" became synonymous with adjectives such as dirty, lazy, and dishonest. Anglos even regarded Mexicans as nonpersons. Folklorist J. Frank Dobie noted in the 1940s how, "Many of the first cowboys thought no more of killing a Mexican than of 'upping' an Indian or using the double of a rope on a rattlesnake."[21] The story of a mass murder in 1842 underscores the racial considerations that defined the place of Tejanos in Victoria that now existed:

> During the year 1842 seven Mexicans came from Camargo, on the Rio Grande, to the mission of Refugio, from which place they despatched [*sic*] a messenger to the mayor of Victoria, Wigington, asking permission to visit Mr. Ysidore Benavides at his ranch on the Chocolate. The mayor readily complying with their wishes, the party proceeded to their destination. One of the number was a brother of Mrs. Benavides, and he brought her some money to which she was entitled from her father's estate. They had also some fine "Mexican blankets" and other articles of Mexican manufacture, which they purposed bartering for tobacco and other articles.[22]

After their visit in Victoria, these seven were ambushed at their encampment about thirty miles to the south of Goliad by Mabry "Mustang" Gray and his company of bandits. Gray and his men killed six of the party and divided their goods and money. The perpetrators left a seventh for dead, but the survivor made his way to Victoria and told his tale to locals who were "horror-stricken at the outrage."[23] But they did not see fit to chase after Gray and his men, apparently viewing the killing of Mexicans as unworthy of concern and justice.

Hostility toward Tejanos in the decade before the Civil War was blatant and still readily apparent to visitors. During his trip through Texas in 1853 Frederick Law Olmsted stayed overnight at the home of a Victoria plantation owner. According to the woman of the household, "White folks and Mexicans were never made to live together anyhow, and the Mexicans had no business here. They were getting so impertinent, and were so well protected by the laws that the Americans would just have to get together and drive them all out of the country." Such attitudes were common in the city, according to Olmsted, who observed that in Victoria, "Mexicans were regarded in a somewhat unchristian tone, not as heretics to be converted with flannel and tracts, but rather as vermin to be exterminated."[24] He further pointed out that, "The Americans are exceedingly suspicious of their vicinity, and drive them off at the least provocation. Those who remain are poor, owning small herds."[25]

As difficult as these conditions were, the late nineteenth century would place Tejanos in a greater quandary as mob action and self-righteous persecution of Mexicans continued. On June 8, 1874, unknown parties murdered an Anglo family from Refugio named Swift. But rumors quickly spread that Mexicans had committed the crime. Local Anglos identified Juan Moya as a suspect as he already held a reputation as a "bad Mexican." A posse led by the Goliad sheriff apprehended Moya, his father, and brother at their home in Victoria County and proceeded to take the men off to jail. But the group of vigilantes that had helped the sheriff in capturing Moya had different ideas for the accused.

A lot of us, however, did not propose to put off a punishment that we knew the Mexicans deserved. The guard and prisoners had gone only about three miles when we surrounded them. The guard offered practically no interference, and in the melee that followed, Marcelo was shot dead. Old Moyer [*sic*] was wounded and down on the ground. A maddened ranch boy rode his plunging horse over him at the same time emptying his six-shooter at him, without effect. Another man dismounted and cut the Mexican's throat with a butcher knife. Antonio Moyer [*sic*] . . . had his arm shot off and was soon dispatched.[26]

Meanwhile, another group of seventy-plus Anglo men had gathered and planned to kill every Mexican in town as vengeance for the Swift murders. Fortunately for the Mexican residents of Goliad, an Anglo named George Saunders quelled the crowd's rage.[27]

At the same time that such aforementioned sentiments relegated Mexicans to a lower status, economic forces worked to further marginalize them. During the post–Civil War years Victoria experienced unprecedented economic growth fueled by expansion both in agriculture and ranching. Cotton production, which had been on the rise in the years immediately preceding the Civil War, declined from 2,212 bales in 1860 to 205 bales in 1870. The industry in the region picked up again during the last thirty years of the century. But the city's future lay in livestock, as indeed, by 1875 Victoria had become a leader in the Texas cattle industry. Victoria ranchers supplied herds to Abilene, Kansas, and other parts of the Midwest.[28] By 1880 Victoria County had 75,000 head of cattle worth over $1 million.[29] Most of those who profited from the new economic direction were Anglo.

During this period (and continuing until the turn of the century) a handful of Anglo families became the town's elite leadership, having profited from cattle ranching and real estate. One such individual was Thomas O'Connor who came to Texas from County Wexford, Ireland, in 1834 with his uncle James Power, one of the founders of the Powers-Hewetson Irish colony in present day Refugio and San Patricio counties. Two years later, at the age of seventeen, O'Connor was the youngest participant in the famous Battle of San Jacinto. In 1838 he married Mary Fagan and combined her small dowry of cattle with land holdings — that he had received in repayment for military service during the revolution — to form the core of a cattle empire that he sold for $140,000 in 1873. He then invested that money in ranch land, eventually acquiring over a half-million acres in Refugio, Aransas, Goliad, San Patricio, McMullen, and La Salle counties. At the time of his death in 1887 he was widely reported to be the single largest property and cattle owner in Texas with an estate worth $4.5 million.[30]

Another important figure who influenced Victoria's economy was James McFaddin who purchased land in Victoria County in 1878. He was one of the first ranchers in Texas to breed and raise Brahman cattle. In 1883, McFaddin, O'Connor, and other investors established in Victoria a meat-packing plant with a workforce of seventy-five butchers. The plant was later moved to Ft. Worth, likely because by the turn of the century Cowtown was becoming a primary transportation center for the cattle industry in the state. In 1888 and 1897 respectively he helped establish a Building and Loan Association and invested in the Guadalupe Valley railroad (a short-lived failure). By the time of his death in 1916 McFaddin had become one of the wealthiest ranchers in the county.[31]

Other individuals responsible for building Victoria's economic foundation in the late nineteenth century were John Newbanks Keeran, Henry Clay Koontz, and John James Welder. Keeran purchased 30,000 acres in Victoria County in 1867. He later was a founder of Victoria National Bank.[32] Koontz was the son of a Swiss immigrant who established a prosperous ranch in Victoria County in 1870. Welder had business interests in cattle raising, pioneered a program of tick eradication, invested in early cotton production, engaged in silo construction, financed Victoria's early light and ice plants, and undertook several road-building projects.[33]

The growth of the economy led local leaders to be confident enough about the future as to investigate the possibility of a modernized infrastructure, specifically, a rail line that would connect Victoria to the coast on one side, and to distant markets through San Antonio on the other. The San Antonio and Mexican Gulf Railway had already constructed a leg from Port Lavaca on the coast to Victoria as early as 1860. Although the line was destroyed during the Civil War it was rebuilt after 1865. By March of 1873 the railway had been expanded farther northwest from Victoria to Cuero. But the railway was abandoned in 1876 partially as a result of the Panic of 1873 but also due to a hurricane that destroyed the port city of Indianola in 1875 (Indianola had replaced Port Lavaca as the major sea outlet between Houston and Corpus Christi). In 1880, however, the New York, Texas and Mexican Railroad began constructing a new line from Rosenberg, Texas (south of Houston), to Victoria; it was finished in 1882 by 600 Italian immigrants, earning it the appellation the "macaroni railroad." The track was purchased in 1883 by the Southern Pacific Railroad, which acquired all smaller rail connections to the Coastal Bend by the end of the century so that Victoria had by 1900 ready access to outside markets via the locomotive.[34]

The step toward modernization accompanied another economic shift underway during the last decade of the nineteenth century. Although cattle remained a significant enterprise in the local economy, the 1890s witnessed the revival of large-scale agricultural production. Because of technological changes and improved techniques, in 1900 the county harvested a record 490,080 bushels of corn and 9,459 bales of cotton. Such dramatic strides in commercial farming continued until the Second World War.[35]

Anglo economic power, needless to say, translated into political hegemony as the mayor's office, the city council, and the county commissioners' court were all dominated exclusively by Anglos. With an entrenched Anglo elite controlling the local economy and monopolizing city and county politics, patterns of discrimination and marginalization against Mexican Americans persisted.

Such turn of events indicated the extent to which a Mexican colony had been transformed into an American city after 1836. Originally, interracial cooperation at least between Mexicans and Irish settlers was obtained in the settlement. But the Texas Revolution produced urges for revenge on Tejanos by Texians for the atrocities at the Alamo and Goliad, and those impulses begot negative stereotypes that came to be commonly accepted. As Crimm has noted, "Mexican Americans had become a separate and distinct entity by 1880, an enclave of Mexican culture among the Anglo, Irish, and German Americans."[36]

Little of consequence changed early in the next century as racial segmentation remained the norm, as did economic subordination. Since an important part of this work involves an understanding of Victoria's cityscape, a brief description of its geography (and its segregationist patterns) is in order. The downtown area today is bounded by Moody Street at the Guadalupe River, north along Moody to North Street, east along North Street to Main Street, and south along Main Street to Water Street. The area generally referred to as the south side covers the broader expanse around and including downtown as bounded by the Guadalupe River west to West Street, then north to

North Street, east along North Street to Navarro Street, then south along Navarro to the Missouri Pacific rail line. The "southeast" refers to all the other areas south of Rio Grande and east of Navarro. The central area refers to the land between Rio Grande Boulevard from Bluff and North Main streets on the west, and to Sam Houston Street on the east. North refers to all the areas north of Sam Houston and Highway 59. For consistency, these are the definitions used throughout the rest of the book.

Through the twentieth century the city gradually grew to the north along Main Street (Highway 87), Rio Grande (Highway 59), and Navarro (Hallettsville Highway, or Highway 77). Leading that movement were Anglo businesses and housing additions. To be sure, Mexican Americans followed the Anglo migration patterns but always lagged several years behind. As Anglos continued moving farther and farther away, Mexican Americans moved into previously Anglo-dominated neighborhoods. Over time, the city became predominantly African American and Mexican American in the southern and eastern parts of town, overwhelmingly Anglo in the northern part of town, and somewhat integrated in the center.

Class distinctions also characterized these geographic zones. The city's Anglo middle and upper classes occupied the north.[37] This left working-class Anglos to dominate the central portions of the city and to experience a measure of integration, albeit primarily with Mexican Americans. African Americans remained largely segregated in the south and east sides. Even as they attempted to move to the central portions of the city in the 1960s and 1970s blacks found themselves generally confined to the Queen City area.

For the most part, segregation mirrored economic disabilities. Until the World War II years, Victoria's economy was firmly rooted in farming and ranching, dominated by Anglo-Americans. The *City Directory* for 1900–01 indicates clearly how the city's retail, service, and financial sectors were all controlled by Anglos as well. Of the 346 businesses the directory listed, only two (or .006 percent) were clearly identifiable as being Mexican American owned. The directory hints at nothing indicating the presence of a Mexican American middle class at the turn of the century. If middle class standing would embrace such traditionally male occupations as managers, clerks, merchants, grocers, and architects, then only one Mexican American male is shown as a manager. Interestingly enough, several African Americans males do show up in the 1900–01 directory: one clerk, two barbers, one professor, and one school instructor. Additionally, there were two female African American teachers. By contrast, the directory listed 105 Anglo males in the above noted occupations. It further contained the names of only twenty-one women employed in traditional female professions (dressmakers, teacher, hotel owner, and clerk), all of whom were Anglo.[38] Mexican Americans earned their livelihoods as farm or ranch hands, as common laborers, or for a lucky few as clerks of sundry types.

Despite such a seemingly dismal economic state for Mexicans, Victoria's economy still attracted immigrants. Newcomers from Mexico arrived in Victoria between 1908 and 1917. Although there is little information about Victoria's early-twentieth-century Mexican immigrants, it is clear that they were about evenly split in terms of literacy. Not all Victoria's immigrants were campesinos, furthermore. Seemingly, many were educated to some degree, and therefore, skilled enough for middle-class status.[39] Regardless of their background, these immigrants found little economic opportunity. Instead, they encountered a hostile social environment that had been in existence since the 1830s. The historical myths of Anglo superiority and Mexican inferiority that were bred during the Texas Revolution and Mexican War persisted, still carrying the same cultural charge that they had in the nineteenth century. Like the members of the old Mexican families of Victoria, Mexican immigrants were seen as lacking in ambition, intelligence, and character.[40]

Unlike nativists in other parts of the country at the time, however, Victoria's Anglos focused almost exclusively on racial characteristics imputed to Mexicans. The antiradical hysteria and religious bigotry that prevailed in other parts of the United States were not factors for the Mexican Catholics of Victoria and much of Texas for several reasons. The American Catholic community failed to greet Mexican Catholics with open arms; by doing so it stifled fears of a wave of Mexican Catholics crossing the border to join American Catholics in usurping Protestant American institutions.[41] Additionally, there existed a substantial Catholic presence among prominent Victorians, including many of the area's leading families. Residence by Irish Catholic immigrants who helped develop Victoria and surrounding counties in the nineteenth century seemingly neutralized the type of large-scale protest against Catholics that erupted in the Northeast and Midwest.

Notions of citizenship race and attendant implications for citizenship, however, were flexible enough to be applied to Germans. Yet as the following case shows, Anglo-Americans were far more forgiving of those that qualified as "whites" than those who did not.

During the war, the local Council of Defense argued in a propaganda pamphlet entitled "Sixty Years of Germany in America," that no "brain can think good, honest, United States patriotism in German words." The pamphlet went on to state that, "There is no genuine honest American household where the English language stops at the front gate." [42] The Council then sought to prohibit the use of the German language in public and private, including services at the Trinity Evangelical Lutheran Church. When, in 1918, parishioners attempted to challenge this decision by virtue of the fact that many older parishioners only spoke German and that their sons were in Europe at that moment fighting to protect U.S. freedom of speech and religion, the Council promptly rejected their claim. [43] In the minds of the Council, and most Anglo Victorians, true citizenship meant abandoning the ways of the old country and embracing a new American identity, an identity that could only be properly expressed in the English language.

Such vehement anti-Germanism illustrates how racial constructions and their relationship to definitions of citizenship can be fluid in nature. Except for a brief period before and during the Civil War, Germans had been welcomed heartily to South Texas. They had enjoyed full benefits of citizenship including opportunities for economic mobility and political activism. Yet for a brief window of time, because of World War I, nationalistic Victorians shaped a narrow definition of citizenship informed by xenophobia and parochialism. In response to this reactionism, Trinity Evangelical Lutheran Church explained that younger church members spoke primarily, if not exclusively, English and that German services would likely die out on their own in a few years. In offering such assurance, the German Lutheran community conceded willingness to see its native tongue abandoned in pursuit of inclusion.

After the war, however, all changed, as German Americans were swiftly reidentified as "American." The entire matter pointed to the malleable nature of race and its implications for understandings of citizenship. In the xenophobia of World War I, Germans had been required to prove their worth by abandoning more rapidly than normal their linguistic attachment to a foreign culture. But once things simmered down, it was again accepted that white German Americans had the quintessence of citizenship (e.g., work ethic, a sense of responsibility, and competence).

The German affair showed how citizenship could be gained on the basis of proving one's willingness to embrace and exhibit white core ideological traits. Mexican Americans were willing to do this, in principle, but they were not generally desirous of abandoning, immediately, all aspects of their cultural identity. Unlike German Lutherans, Mexican Americans were accepting of what was considered white public (political, economic, legal, educational) culture, but were less inclined to forsake their private (home, neighborhood, church, language) identity.

Nonetheless, the experiences of World War I and the national unity it created contributed significantly to the Americanization of Mexican Americans. Throughout the state, Mexican Americans joined the military during World War I, motivated by a sense of patriotism and a resolve to escape the wrenching poverty of farm and ranch life. Whether fighting on battlefields in Europe or taking part in civic activities on the home front, many Mexican Americans of differing classes approached the War as an exercise in civic duty. Some Mexican Americans expressed their patriotism by collecting money for flags, while others worked with the Red Cross, and many engaged in Liberty Bond drives. Thus, the war experience ignited a new sense of Americanism within many Mexican Americans. One result of this changing consciousness was the postwar emergence of several new organizations such as the Order of Sons of America in San Antonio, which merged with other similar organizations in 1929 to create the League of United Latin American Citizens (LULAC).[44] Unfortunately, any postwar hopes for progress by Mexican Americans in their quest for equality were interrupted by the economic burdens brought on by the Great Depression.

The Depression marked an important turning point for Mexican Americans' consciousness in seemingly contradictory ways. First, it further limited Mexican Americans' expectations of upward economic mobility. Yet other Mexican Americans, such as those who joined LULAC, began rethinking their status as Mexicans who happened to be living in America. Historian Mario T. García has argued that it was a time when, throughout the country, children of those who came in the immigrant waves before the Depression reached political age. From about 1930 to the mid-1960s, he argues, Mexicans sought ways to find a place for themselves in American society as American citizens.

By the 1930s Mexican Americans in Victoria were moving toward a bicultural identity, hoping for acceptance, as had the local German population by the 1920s. They were, for instance, increasingly developing a working knowledge of the English language. In Victoria, 326 out of 366 Mexican American heads of household in 1933 spoke English.[45] Certainly this was not out of step with English proficiency among the German community that only fifteen years prior had been persecuted for holding religious services in German. Indeed, a pattern of gradually increasing English language skills is perceptible within Victoria's Spanish-speaking community during the Depression period. There also seems to have surfaced a gradual, albeit grudging, realization by the white community that Mexican Americans were in fact adopting the same outlooks that Anglos associated with full citizenship.

Enduring practices of segregation and discrimination clashed with recognitions of Mexican American acculturation to produce paradoxical situations. In 1936 the city of Victoria scheduled a centennial celebration that included a dance at Pleasure Island (a complex consisting of a swimming pool, roller skating rink, and dance hall) that was off-limits to nonwhites.[46] Yet the parade that accompanied the celebration had Félix de León, the great-great-great grandson of the city's founder, Don Martín de León, as the color bearer.[47] The seeming incongruity between organized segregated festivities and a parade that included an honorable acknowledgement of the city's Mexican history was an example of the ways in which white elites in Victoria traditionally sustained a strong sense of selective historical memory and enforced racialist notions of citizenship. White and Mexican citizens cherished the memory of the city's Mexican founder Martín de León, and perhaps whites thought it time to concede that Mexicans merited recognition as Americans. The decision might have been made easier since de León was popularly remembered as Spanish (he was in fact a criollo, of pure Spanish blood), rather than Mexican. Hence, he was different from the mestizo bloodline that defined the contemporary Mexican American community and that now was accepting American normative behavior.

If Anglo-Americans in Victoria before World War II had relied on the uncertain future of farming and ranching (with Mexican immigrant labor as its relief) their economic destiny took a marked turn during the 1940s with the large-scale exploitation of oil. Intentional extraction of oil for market purposes first occurred on December 1, 1931, on the McFaddin ranch, which immediately began producing 500 barrels daily. In 1932 Victoria County produced over 9,000 barrels yearly. By 1935 the county topped the half-million barrel mark and reached production levels of 4.8 million barrels annually in 1938–39.[48] With the emergence of oil production in Victoria county, the oil industry during the WWII years came to dominate the area's economy and marked the first major step toward increased industrialization. After oil was discovered in Bloomington in 1947, oil production became a vital part of the area's economy and it was only a matter of time before the petrochemical industry moved into the area.[49]

In 1951 the Aluminum Company of America (Alcoa) began building a $30 million plant thirty miles to the southeast of Victoria in Calhoun County. That same year, E. I. DuPont de Nemours and Co., opened a plant in southern Victoria County.[50] Four years later Union Carbide announced that it would be building a $60 million plant in Seadrift, Texas (a nearby community), providing employment to hundreds of men in Victoria.[51]

The Golden Crescent area attracted petrochemical producers for several reasons. Such plants required access to water transportation, and this was made available by the barge canal. The Golden Crescent also offered an affordable labor force with a very weak tradition of union activity. Thus, petrochemical companies could build in the region and realize easy access to larger ports without concern about a serious threat by organized labor.[52]

During the 1950s the major petrochemical plants, even those located outside the county, provided a significant boost to the local economy through payrolls. Between 1950 and 1960, 38 percent of all Alcoa employees lived in the city of Victoria and spent much of their earnings therein. The vast majority of DuPont employees (80 percent) resided in Victoria County, and over half of those lived within the city limits. Similarly, 84 percent of Union Carbide employees made the daily commute from Victoria County. These numbers remained fairly constant through subsequent decades.[53] Meanwhile, another large employer, the federal government, reestablished a military presence in the city. In the fall of 1951 the military reopened Foster Field as a training base for Korean War pilots, and its presence provided yet another stimulus to the local economy that lasted well after the war; the base contributed over $1 million in salaries alone in 1957.[54]

Because of the influx of new petrochemical and military industries the city's population grew from 11,566 in 1940 to 16,126 by 1950, and then to 33,047 in 1960.[55] In 1930, 50 percent of all gainfully employed people in Victoria County worked in some type of agricultural concern, 20 percent in industry, 18 percent in the service sector, and 12 percent in banking and insurance. By 1960, however, less than 2 percent of workers in Victoria County were employed in agriculture, whereas the industrial sector (including construction trades) and service industries now accounted for 90 percent of all employment in the area. Victoria County in a brief thirty years had thus become an industrial and urbanized community. The transformation did not circumvent Mexican Americans; by the 1950s they too were becoming predominantly an urban people.

But the petrochemical boom did not directly benefit Mexican Americans. Employment discrimination led to higher-paying skilled jobs for Anglos; Mexican Americans by contrast, saw relegation to low-wage, unskilled jobs in attendant industries and in the service sector positions available in the oil business and petrochemical plants. Despite the undesirability of such work, Mexican Americans still saw these limited opportunities as a chance to move into town in the hopes of eventually surmounting the constraints of rural life and providing their children with better schools. The magnetic effect of this trend toward Mexican American urbanization, meanwhile, had profound effects on the barrio. Not only did it grow in size and population but it also experienced a transformation from a quiet center of Mexican American culture into the city's red light district.[56] Paradoxically, in the midst of Anglo prosperity Mexican Americans saw their own neighborhoods become more crowded and deteriorated.

The economic changes of the 1940s and 1950s hardly tempered entrenched racial ideology, as seen in the fact that even American servicemen of Mexican background faced continued discrimination. In September of 1952, Fausto Ramírez, a highly decorated thirty-year-old World War II veteran, was assigned to Foster Air Base as an employee of the Army Corps of Engineers. His job was to process modifications to government contracts worth over one-half million dollars. Upon arriving in the city he approached the Victoria Chamber of Commerce for assistance finding housing for his family, but was given the discouraging news that "furnished apartments were scarce . . . and that those [he] found would rent high." As he searched on his own most landlords explained that they had no vacancies even though they had placed ads in the newspaper. He eventually found an apartment on East River Street, but on September 13 (two days after moving in), the landlord refunded his money declaring: "You will have to move out immediately. I did not know that you people were Mexicans and we do not rent to Mexicans so pick up your things and move out immediately." The landlord added that the presence of Ramírez and his family was "bothering the American families living here." Ramírez relocated his wife to Laredo (where they were originally from) and rented a room for himself at the home of Pedro Gonzales at 1709 E. Juan Linn St.[57]

Because of such vestiges of the past, the Victoria Mexican American community came to be integrated into the larger network of investigations being conducted by groups such as the American G.I. Forum (AGIF) and the Good Neighbor Commission (GNC). Ed Idar, chairman of the AGIF, learned of the Ramírez incident and contacted Vaughn Bryant of the Good Neighbor Commission. In his letter Idar said:

> Apparently in Victoria there is no distinction as to the educational, professional, social, or economic position of the people of Mexican descent that are subjected to discrimination. This is one of the worst cases to come to my attention and is certainly a black mark against the community in question.[58]

But Ramírez's experience was not the only example of residential discrimination. In May 1952 the Victoria Housing Authority announced plans to develop additional accommodations for "Latin-Americans and Negroes in the low-income brackets." The announcement, printed in the *Houston Post* on May 4, caught the attention of Ed Idar, who pro-

Club Westerner. This dance hall was part of the larger entertainment complex, which contained the swimming pool the Mexican American Brownie Troop was turned away from in the 1950s. Subsequently, Manuel Villafranca purchased the facility and the Club Westerner became an important center for Tejano music. *Courtesy Victoria Regional History Center, Victoria College/UH-Victoria Library*

tested the discriminatory nature of the plan. But no pretense was made to disguise the intention, as Housing Authority executive director W. L. Seiler acknowledged that there were separate units being built specifically for Mexican, African, and Anglo-Americans.[59] The Human Relations Council of Victoria (the local arm of the Good Neighbor Commission manned by local Anglos) paid scant attention to Idar's complaint.[60]

Discrimination as monitored by the Good Neighbor Commission during the 1950s extended to various other fronts. Rib's Cafe (on the Port Lavaca highway) and the Triangle Drive Inn (301 W. Rio Grande) refused service to Mexican American customers. So did the Pleasure

Island swimming pool and skating rink, which denied entry to Mexican American Girl Scouts.[61] But the GNC did little about such problems, mainly because it delegated responsibility to local community leaders who often did not take their roles seriously. A memo concerning the Victoria Human Relations Council (the local branch of the GNC) noted that:

Re: Victoria

There is a thick file on Victoria discrimination going back to 1943. These two papers concern a previous case at Triangle Dive-In [*sic*].

According to Zack [*sic*] Lentz, a prominent resident of Victoria and friend of John Ben Shepperd, Victoria is on the blacklist. I met Zack [*sic*] Lentz casually the other day, asked him if he knew anybody on the HRC in Victoria. He acted as though he didn't know there was one. This is odd, because one of the members of it is named Cody Lentz [his brother].[62]

The lackadaisical attitude local Anglo elites manifested toward Mexican American civil rights issues at midcentury reflected lingering and still widespread tensions between Anglos and Mexican Americans. It would be taken to task beginning in the 1940s and 1950s.

FROM 1836 and lasting through the mid-twentieth century, the city of Victoria grew and the region around it became progressively industrialized. During the 1940s and 1950s Mexican Americans left the farms and ranches in the areas around Victoria in search of better work and improved education for their children in the city, as did other Mexican Americans around the nation. Instead of new opportunities, however, most faced employment and housing discrimination. The old barrio itself expanded, for therein was to be found the least expensive accommodations for the newcomers from the countryside.

In the meantime, Victoria's Mexican Americans had during the interwar period developed and nurtured a sense of themselves as American citizens deserving of equal social and political standing. This evolving American identity would bubble to the surface of the community's collective consciousness about the time of the Second World War when Mexican Americans organized and launched an activist challenge to the limits of ethnic progress. Motivated by the contradictions between the tenets of the Constitution, the principles of the Declaration of Independence, and the mythical promises of popular ideology on one hand, and the realities of segregation and discrimination on the other, Mexican Americans would in the postwar years delineate a clear vision of their idea of citizenship. They did so by employing limited forms of resistance, namely mainstream political reforms and the courts, and tactics generally identified with Mexican American activism of the 1940s and 1950s and ones that stand in marked contrast to the manifestations of activism in the Chicano era of the 1960s and 1970s.

In Victoria, as elsewhere, this vision for a place in its American promise would be ensconced in an ideological framework that embraced the fundamental aspects of American political-economy. It involved an activism that mirrored the behavior and approaches of national organizations such as LULAC and AGIF, both of which fought through the ballot box and the judicial system to end discriminatory employment, social segregation, substandard housing, and inferior educational conditions. Mexican Americans in Victoria would likewise claim the role of the patriotic social critics taking unprecedented interests in the education of youths, and in lending greater support to benevolent and civic organizations. They would embark on a course of resistance that appears on the surface to be rather conservative, compliant, and accommodationist. This work argues, however, that in reality such behavior logically emanated from an evolving bifurcated Mexican American identity that at once embraced a public identity informed by acceptance of attitudes defined by the mainstream as normative while retaining a more personal identity steeped in Mexican culture.

"For God, for Country, for Home"

The Catholic Church and Mexican American Identity Formation

T HE ROOTS of the Catholic faith in Victoria, Texas, can be traced to the founding of the city by empresario Don Martín de León in 1824 when his colonists erected a Catholic church in the central town square. While many Anglo settlers who moved to the Victoria area before, during, and after the Texas Revolution were Protestants from the southern United States, a constant Catholic presence obtained throughout the 1800s due to the residence of Tejanos, as well as of Irish, Czech, and German immigrants.[1] But even as Victoria's racial landscape came to resemble the rest of the state, its white Catholics (even the Irish) never faced the type of bigotry experienced by other Catholic ethnic groups such as Mexicans (and Italians elsewhere). Many of the leading white Catholic families in the city (such as the Welders and O'Connors), for instance, became wealthy community leaders by the early twentieth century and in so doing proved themselves worthy of equal citizenship. Mexican American Catholics, by contrast, remained poor, largely uneducated, and the victims of racism and attendant discrimination throughout the nineteenth and twentieth centuries. In Victoria, as in other parts of the state, racial chauvinism superseded religious bigotry.

By the 1910s the city's two Catholic churches (St. Mary's Parish, established in 1840, and Our Lady of Lourdes, established in 1875) served the needs of Victoria's Catholic community but did not provide sufficient resources for a growing Mexican American presence. Hence, Anglo parishioners at St. Mary's in 1913 opened a mission annex for the town's "Mexicans" (the auxiliary mission would be under the oversight of St. Mary's council). Originally named Mission Dolores, the church soon became the site of controversy as Mexican Americans wished to be able to name their own place of worship. A compromise was quickly reached, so that the name became Our Lady of Sorrows (Nuestra Señora de Dolores, which, over time, became a separate parish in its own right). This early contest over what to call the sanctuary foreshadowed other disputes, especially around the time of World War II, during which Our Lady of Sorrows (OLS) would play an important role in the processes of Mexican American identity formation and expression in Victoria.[2]

The Catholic Church overall took a paternalistic view of Mexican Americans during the early part of the century. The Church, nationally, was dedicated to the goal of assimilating its immigrant flock, and saw newly arriving people from Mexico in need of spiritual as well as secular amelioration. For Mexican Americans in Victoria, the early years of the century appear to have been marked by a narrowly defined relationship that centered on sacramental duties.

Later in the century the Church became more flexible, allowing for parishioners' self-expression. By the 1940s, indeed, Mexican Americans began to see the Church as an agent for the negotiation of Mexican American identity and culture, and for carving out a niche for themselves in the larger society. Ultimately, by the end of the 1980s, a new archbishop, and two socially conscious Sisters, would attempt to bring about significant changes in the material conditions of Victoria's working class in general, and its Mexican Americans in particular. These efforts would cause the Church to take a sharp turn from an attitude of paternalistic condescension to one of compassion and shared destiny.[3]

ORIGINALLY, Catholics from all ethnic groups in Victoria, as in other Texas communities, worshiped alongside Anglos. Although it is not clear how many total parishioners were affiliated with St. Mary's Parish at the turn of the century, the 1910 Annual Parish Report noted the presence of 132 American families, twenty-five Italian families, and thirty-two single individuals (widows, widowers, maids, etc.) for a total of 778 souls. But the report noted that the figures did not reflect Mexicans: their total could only be computed by noting the number of baptisms that year, and that amounted to 119. By comparison, there had been thirty-four American and eight Italian baptisms, according to the survey.[4] Evidently, the number of Mexicans in the parish continued to grow, and so by the 1910s Anglos laid plans to build a separate mission church.

The practice of developing segregated parishes did not originate in Victoria. In San Benito, Texas, a Catholic church had originally been established in 1910 on the Mexican side of town because most of the faithful were Mexicanos. Both Anglos and Mexicans attended mass there, but did not do so in harmony. Due to the fact that most parishioners were Mexican, masses were generally held in Spanish. Separate Anglo and Mexican choirs existed. Cultural differences in faith practices produced conflicting ideas concerning the ornamentation of the church. Mexicans presented the local priest with a statue of Our Lady of Guadalupe while Anglos one of St. Ann. In 1911, Anglos raised money to erect their own separate church, which they called St. Francis.[5] Similarly, in 1912 Anglo Catholics from St. Mary's in Victoria argued that perhaps it might be better if the "Mexicans" had their own site where they could be ministered to in their own language. The proposed edifice was to be constructed on the city's south side where it would be of convenience to the barrio.[6]

Frank Welder, a prominent community leader and millionaire, contributed three-fourths of the funds required for construction of the new Mexican mission. Other anonymous donors joined him and together they raised the necessary $4,000 for the new structure. In response, the diocese honored Welder's request that the establishment be named Mission Dolores in honor of his mother, Dolores Welder.[7] Along with clergy and Anglo benefactors, prospective parishioners were invited to the festivities surrounding the mission's opening. Church correspondence indicates the views the Church held toward its Mexican flock as Father F. X. Heck, pastor of St. Mary's, notified Reverend J. W. Shaw of San Antonio about plans for the event: "We will send word to the Mexicans and have everything ready for your Lordship."[8] By this time the word "Mexican" had acquired a pejorative meaning and was widely used in that context. The lack of an alternative phrase such as "Latin Americans," or "the Spanish-speaking," indicated that Father Heck employed the same language as his Anglo parishioners. That language pointed to the state of race relations in the city: "us" meant white Americans while Mexicans represented the "other." This aside, the church building was officially dedicated on December 21, 1913, the Sunday before Christmas.

Within four years, however, the parishioners of Mission Dolores sought to become an autonomous parish and asked to call their church by something that would reflect their own identity rather than one designated by the local Anglo elite. But such efforts to rename the church upset Frank Welder. Ultimately, the two parties reached a compromise by which the church would be named Our Lady of Sorrows (Nuestra Señora de Dolores).[9] Reverend Baque, the parish priest for OLS, was happy ministering at Nuestra Señora de Dolores because the name was popular among Catholics in Spain.[10]

At the same time that the Catholic Church created the Mexican mission, it also established an attendant education facility. Dubbed Guadalupe School, it was established to serve Mexican American children in Victoria who could not afford the tuition at Nazareth Academy, the only other similar parochial establishment in town.[11] Anglo Catholics believed that such an institution was necessary because, due to language barriers, local Mexican American Catholics had "neglected their [children's] spiritual worship."[12] But the Catholic Church sought to go beyond spiritual uplift and used the mission school as a tool of acculturation to help make up for the perceived linguistic and cultural deficiencies of school age Mexicanos. Thus, along with traditional instruction in religion, students were trained in secular subjects like mathematics and English, as well as in citizenship, politeness, and respect for others.[13] These were lessons that the Church assumed to be missing from the daily lived experience of Mexicano children. Mexican American children presumably descended from culturally deprived homes wherein a "backward" Mexican culture failed to impart proper American values such as the work ethic, cleanliness, fair play, responsibility, and patriotism.

Anglo priests only grudgingly ministered to Victoria's Mexicanos. In 1914 priests from St. Mary's were still being assigned to assist Reverend Baque in his full-time duties at Our Lady of Sorrows. Father Heck, the

Our Lady of Sorrows Mexican mission church erected 1913. *Courtesy Sofia Postel Wilson*

pastor of St. Mary's, sought the advice of Reverend J. W. Shaw in San Antonio concerning a Father Zuber whom Heck noted had shown great interest in local work, but "I do not believe that he likes the idea of being selected for Mexican missions." [14]

Father Heck and his flock's views toward Mexicans was further evidenced in January, 1917, when Heck wrote to Reverend Shaw regarding one Reverend Pueyo who had been assigned to St. Mary's' Parish. Heck stated:

> I have absolutely no objection to Rev. Pueyo and think that he is a good and holy man, but you cannot but see that he is of so little help for St. Mary's church. Quite a number have told me that they do not understand him and he does not understand them in the confessional. Your Lordship yourself remarked that you do not understand the good man. Sanctity and being suitable for a place are two different things, [*sic*] It is true that the good man is making a heroic effort, but I am afraid that he is too old to change his dictum and ways, and I cannot blame the altar boys and many others for bursting into laughter when he makes an attempt at English. Letting him read the Gospel and make announcement in case that my throat would be bad on Sunday is entirely out of question, and what about the extra instructions and the approaching extra work for Lent. Now I am not finding fault with any of your arrangements or with the Rev. Father, whom I consider a very good man, but I am simply stating the facts that confront me in the parish work. If your Lordship still maintains that you cannot change conditions — very well, I will do all that I can do, and as long as I can ward off throat trouble. If however my throat fails, I will never make another attempt.[15]

Shaw wrote back to Heck indicating that he was searching for a replacement to assist at St. Mary's and might consider sending Pueyo to OLS.[16]

The Catholic hierarchy itself tended to reinforce racial segregation in Victoria. In 1943, for example, Archbishop Robert E. Lucey of San Antonio appointed the Reverend Daniel E. Giorgi to be pastor of Our Lady of Sorrows Parish. In his appointment letter, Lucey informed Giorgi that, "you are appointed Pastor of the Parish of Our Lady of Sorrows in Victoria, having jurisdiction over all Mexican People in the county of Victoria."[17] Unlike other parishes, OLS had no physical boundaries: its own delineations were racial in nature. Over time, as the city grew, controversies arose from time to time over geographical lines between new parishes. But it was always understood that OLS was responsible for ministering to Mexican Catholics throughout the region.[18] By taking such a jaundiced approach, the Catholic Church functioned hand-in-hand with secular institutions that held Mexican Americans in a condition of second-class citizenship. The assignment problems involving Fathers Zuber and Pueyo further confirmed that the Church reflected the wider racist tendencies across the city and country. But as long as Mexican Americans had a place wherein to worship and practice their beliefs in their own ways, they found strength in their faith and a sanctuary for cultural nourishment. In this private space, they could, for instance, pay homage to *la virgen* (the Virgin Mary). Ironically, segregated churches often became training grounds for the marginalized to hone leadership skills.

Even though Our Lady of Sorrows emerged out of a pattern of discrimination in a segregated society, parishioners turned to the Church as a source of pride and claimed it as their own in both spiritual and secular terms. One manifestation of this spirit occurred in 1944 when they selected a Mexican American contractor, Lupe Robles, a parishioner whose workers were also Mexican American, to construct a new parish hall. Robles agreed to charge no more than $1.00 an hour for his own work, while the Church insisted on Robles paying workers the prevailing union wages.[19] For parishioners, having one of their own build the new hall offered a sense of empowerment and agency and made this new part of the parish truly theirs in a most fundamental way — they (through Robles) actually built it.

Apparently there was some question as to the capability of Robles and his men to complete the job satisfactorily, for Father Beck of St. Mary's looked into Mr. Robles's credentials. It is not clear why the pastor of St. Mary's became involved in the issue of securing a builder for the Mexican Parish Hall. Conceivably, on the one hand Beck was looking out for the interests of Anglo contractors. On the other hand Archbishop Robert E. Lucey's assistant, the Reverend James T. Lockwood, was perhaps concerned about the ability of a Mexican contractor to be trusted with such an important project. Whatever the case may have been, Beck suggested that Father Giorgi, the pastor of OLS, had faith in the ability of Robles and his staff to complete the job. As Beck put it, "Incidentally, his group, i.e. Father Giorgi's, stick together and don't

Opposite Above, OLS in the 1930s. The Church had become physically larger to accommodate the growing parish. Below, a side view of the same church. *Courtesy Sofia Postel Wilson*

suffer from an inferiority complex by any means. I would advise, therefore, to approve Mr. Robles as the man for the job." [20] Lucey agreed to allow Robles to do the work. [21]

By December 12, 1944, OLS sought to add a rectory to accompany the Church structure and indicated to the Archdiocese that it held in hand $5,000 for such purposes. Reverend Lockwood, assistant to Archbishop Lucey, wondered how the money had been raised, or if it had been borrowed. Pastor Giorgi notified Lockwood that the parishioners themselves had collected the money. Giorgi further noted:

> Perhaps the only conclusion that might be offered for any relatively rapid financial rise may be that the past eighteen months found the Latin-Americans of Victoria County properly provided with an "all-out" spiritual assistance. Any apparent neglect in the past by the pastor to raise the financial standing of this parish may have been due either to an insufficient number of priests, or to a lack of priestly interest on the part of those in charge here. [22]

Ultimately, the archbishop allowed Giorgi to complete the building of a new rectory.

THAT THIS BID by Mexican Americans wanting to build the new rectory occurred in the early 1940s is not coincidental, for World War II had the same impact on Mexican Americans nationally and in Victoria as it did in other parts of Texas. The war produced a new sense of self-awareness among many and inspired fresh struggles for citizenship rights. Such a consciousness was expressed in Victoria in the 1940s and afterward through, for example, the effort to build the rectory in 1944, the creation of new Mexican American organizations (as detailed in chapter 4), but more specifically, through animated involvement in Church organizations as well.

There is no record of Mexican American parish activities from 1917 until the early 1940s, aside from sacramental documents and correspondence concerning official Church business such as budgetary issues. Beginning in 1942, however, members of Our Lady of Sorrows began forming parish organizations that exist to the present. These organizations have focused on very different activities and have drawn from diverse segments of the parish population. As such, they have historically developed and expressed varying aspects of the identities of Victoria's Mexican American Catholics. An important function of such societies has been to mix religion and promote the community's Mexicanidad. One such organization was the Guadalupanas.

This first significant long-lasting parish organization was formed in 1942 by women.[23] The notion of a women's organization within a Mexican American parish was neither new nor restricted to Victoria. The Church had traditionally offered women acceptable ways to move outside the home and take on leadership roles normally ascribed to men. It had done this through Church associations such as the Vela Perpetua (perpetual candle) and Las Hijas de María (daughters of Mary), which existed in other parts of the Southwest.

In this tradition, women at Our Lady of Sorrows formed Las Guadalupanas. According to legend, the Virgin Mary appeared to the Indian Juan Diego outside of Mexico City in December, 1531. From that point to the present, the image of the Virgen de Guadalupe has held a prominent place in the hearts and minds of Mexican American (and Mexican) Catholics.[24] In one sense the Guadalupanas was simply another parish organization. It held revenue raisers for the church, assisted other groups with their fundraising activities, and provided a sense of community and importance for their fellow members.[25] But the Guadalupanas are worth noting for two other interrelated reasons.

First, the Guadalupanas offered a way for women to sustain one very valuable aspect of their Mexican identity. Earlier in the twentieth century the Catholic Church, nationally, had attempted to homogenize its "foreign" parishioners, and inculcate them with Anglo-American Catholic middle-class values, presumably because nonwhite cultures were considered frail or in need of improvement through cultural regeneration. Yet the Guadalupanas used their organization to continue celebrating the Catholic tradition and the cult of the virgin in a customary Mexican way.

The Guadalupanas' sense of fulfillment was drawn from a belief that through their activities they were promoting the spiritual purpose of the Church. The highlight of the year for the Guadalupanas of Victoria came each December 12 on the feast day of the Virgen de Guadalupe. They organized a six-block procession from the town plaza to Our Lady of Sorrows where the parish priest offered a high mass in honor of the virgin. The Guadalupanas were the guests of honor at the mass. During the rest of the year they engaged in social activities such as putting on morality plays, in Spanish, for the church members at large. For these women the organization provided a way to fulfill the Church's mission yet in a manner that enhanced their heritage and traditions in the public sphere.

And therein lies the second reason why the Guadalupanas were significant. The organization offered women the opportunity to take on leadership roles. Guadalupanas tended to come from blue-collar households, and frequently did not work outside the home. But church involvement allowed women the room to broaden their traditional boundaries. While this service in the public arena was limited to traditional women's roles as spiritual agents and nurturers, the opportunities permitted women to become decision makers in their own right.[26]

By the 1980s, however, membership in the organization waned.[27] Several reasons explain its decline. For many women, the organization was an extension of Church structure that did not provide openings for challenging male-defined boundaries. In church activities, women perceived a sexual division of labor that mirrored their home lives. The fundraising events the Guadalupanas sponsored tended to center on the sale of food they themselves had prepared. Then, disinterest by the younger generation also weakened the organization. As older members passed away they were not replaced in equal numbers by younger parishioners who had come to increasingly see the Guadalupanas as the province of elderly women.[28] Meanwhile, men took an interest in parallel organizations that would offer them the chance to pursue their spirituality and express their sense of identity. One such individual was Isidore Ozuna.

Isidore Ozuna was born on a ranch in Victoria County on April 30, 1925. As a youth, Ozuna acquired through his family a devotion to the Catholic faith, a belief in the value of education, and a sense of patriotism as an American citizen. In 1943, almost two years after the United States had entered World War II, Ozuna enlisted in the Navy at the tender age of eighteen. He then spent the duration of the war on the battleship *Colorado* in the Pacific theater. After his discharge Ozuna stayed for a time in Milwaukee, Wisconsin, where he attended trade school. But he returned to Victoria permanently in 1953, took a position with the United States Postal Service, and settled down to raise a family.[29]

War veterans such as Ozuna sought ways to express their patriotism as well as their faith, and found it in the Catholic War Veterans (CWV).

On March 12, 1947, veteran parishioners of Our Lady of Sorrows established Post 1269 of the Catholic War Veterans of America. The CWV offered members a satisfaction of belonging, a chance to perform public service, and a medium through which they could promote their vision of Americanism. Unlike other more activist civic organizations that were organized and managed by Mexican Americans (such as the League of United Latin American Citizens and the American G.I. Forum), the CWV of Our Lady of Sorrows functioned within the parameters established by the nonethnically oriented national organization, and this begot a more quiescent view of the relationship of Mexican Americans to American society. Members took pride in the consensual attitude embodied in the CWV motto: "For God, for Country, and for Home!" Just as there was no mention of a quest for social justice in the slogan, neither was there a critique of American society, culture, or politics in the Our Lady of Sorrows CWV Post.[30] This attitude paralleled the position that Mexican American organizations in Victoria took in the postwar years. The American Citizens' Social Club, American G.I. Forum (AGIF), and the de León club similarly refused to challenge the fundamental structure of the American way of life. In the same way as the Catholic Church hierarchy had over the decades endorsed the premises of the American racist social order, so did the CWV mirror a general acceptance of American worldviews.

One important reason for this consensual attitude was the Catholic War Veterans' nonethnic orientation. The CWV was a national organization initially launched in 1935 by World War I veterans in Long Island, New York, generally for the purpose of representing veterans before the Veteran's Administration. Over time CWV had gone on to promote patriotism and the Catholic faith, look after the welfare of widows of war veterans, and wage a battle against communism as well as other forces that posed a threat to America. The Golden Jubilee Souvenir Book published by Our Lady of Sorrows in 1968 to commemorate the fiftieth anniversary of the parish described the CWV thus:

> [CWV members] are united together in order to guard the rights and privileges of veterans, protect our freedom, defend our Faith, help our sick and disabled care for the widows and

orphans of deceased Veterans, promote Americanism and foster Catholic Action. Each CWV member is pledged to a personal and unified warfare against atheistic Communism and all
other groups which are subversive and dangerous to our American form of government.[31]

World War II veterans at Our Lady of Sorrows Parish found such
a patriotic, vehemently anticommunist organization quite appealing.
The CWV offered them a place for expressing their faith, community
spirit, and patriotism, and the setting for passing on these virtues to
fellow Mexican American parishioners. Thus the CWV sponsored a
parish Boy Scout troop as well as softball teams. By so doing it attempted
to foster in Mexican American boys the same kinds of camaraderie and
group values that their generation found necessary to ward off the
threatening forces of totalitarianism. Scholarship money they raised allowed working-class students from the barrio a chance to attend St. Joseph High School, the only Catholic high school in the city.[32]
    While the CWV also expressed a belief in the strength of families,
it abided by a policy of gender discrimination, a practice that corre-
sponded to the sexual divisions extant not only within the Mexican
American community but also within the Catholic Church. Thus the
CWV directed women toward the Ladies Auxiliary, where members
engaged in fundraising events for the maintenance of the church itself or for providing useful items to the local hospitals.[33] Despite real
discriminatory behavior, however, the CWV marked a proud chapter
in the lives of many OLS parishioners, among them Isidore Ozuna.
The organization allowed Mexican American Catholics to focus on
the three most important aspects of their lives: home and family, patriotism, and the Catholic faith. Through participation in the CWV,
Ozuna, other Mexican American veterans, and their allies in the Wom-
en's Auxiliary were able to contribute to the very society and community they embraced as their own: "We [members of the CWV] tried
to keep the youth involved in good American activities and instill [in
them] the Catholic viewpoint," declared Ozuna.[34]
    In the meantime, another organization had been focusing on the
needs of OLS young people. The Catholic Youth Organization (CYO)
in the 1940s and 1950s promoted the Catholic faith among parish youth
and simultaneously acted as a socializing agent. Traditionally, CYO

members attended a monthly CYO mass, raised funds for the church, and organized outings for its members that promoted an aura of Christian fellowship. In no way did the CYO deviate from the ideological consensus promoted by the CWV and other secular Anglo and Mexican American organizations. If anything, the CYO operated to reinforce the same values learned in the public schools and at home. While emphasizing conformity, the organization still aimed to develop a strong feeling of Mexicanidad among its members, however. In the 1960s, indeed, the CYO experienced a dramatic change that would forever alter its designation as simply a place for young people to gather and share their faith.[35] The CYO now became an organization wherein members celebrated their cultural past, and wherein members could connect others to their rediscovered heritage. Interestingly enough, this course that allowed for a new identity was charted almost by accident, when the Guadalupanas asked the youth group to help fill in time during a Guadalupana stage production.

In early 1960 Father Hyacinth Rosati, pastor of Our Lady of Sorrows, asked Elizabeth Sepúlveda if she would mind working with some volunteers from the CYO and put on a brief dance exhibition during an intermission of an upcoming morality play being performed by the Guadalupanas. Sepúlveda had recently relocated to Victoria with her husband Pete who had desired to return to his hometown. Prior to moving to Victoria, however, Sepúlveda had been a professional dancer in San Antonio. In the 1950s she had performed with various dance troupes in Chicago and San Francisco. Sepúlveda's small group put on such an impressive demonstration at the Guadalupana function that it began presenting public exhibitions of a handful of Mexican folk dances. The group usually performed at St. Mary's Parish (the one that had spawned OLS, and which was located a mere four blocks away) auditorium.[36]

Father Vincent Patrizi received a transfer to OLS as assistant pastor in 1961 and got the responsibility of overseeing the CYO. Under his direction the youth group in 1963 staged a larger production entitled "Trip around the World," which included a variety of dances such as the Cha Cha Cha, the Can Can, and the Calypso Dance. Despite the depth of its repertoire, the group desired to focus more specifically on traditional Mexican dances.[37]

Pursuing such specialization the dance company planned a trip to

Nicole Jeanine Gonzales practicing to perform with the OLS Ballet Folklorico, ca. 1987. Youth from elementary through high school developed an appreciation for their culture through the Catholic Youth Organization dance troupe. *Courtesy Victoria Regional History Center, Victoria College/UH-Victoria Library*

Mexico, where it might learn more dances and songs indigenous to various regions of Mexico. Sixty CYO members thus held fundraisers for a bus trip that summer to study dance with the Ballet Folklorico of Mexico City. This sojourn resulted in a consciousness-raising experience. Prior to the trip the students knew little more about Mexico than that the country was located to the south of the United States and that it was the nation from which their families descended. Now they realized that Mexico too had a history; Mexico too had a rich culture worth investigating and celebrating. They learned that their U.S. education had cheated them out of any kind of positive contact with their ethnic past.[38]

Inspired by this trip, the group decided to call itself "Our Lady of Sorrows CYO Ballet Folklorico." For the rest of the decade, the troupe maintained its Mexico City connection. In so doing it funded summers in Mexico City for two members who learned new dances and new songs and then brought them back to Victoria and shared that information with the rest of the Ballet. Due in large part to Father Vincent's promotional skills, the group also traveled the state in the 1960s, gaining national attention in the process. The highpoint for the CYO Ballet Folklorico came in the spring of 1970 when it was invited to perform in Washington, D.C., for President Richard M. Nixon.[39]

The trips to Mexico and the various performances allowed CYO members to celebrate their culture publicly. Participation in the dance ensemble brought them in touch with their roots and gave them a reason to feel pride in their heritage; it also counteracted the embarrassment they felt from daily contact with Anglo society and from school experiences where the only references to Mexicans, Mexico, or Mexican American culture were negative. Most of the teenagers came from a world of Mexican ethnicity, one grounded on a Spanish language home life, familiar Mexican foods, and a Catholic religious upbringing (many of the masses at OLS were still held in Spanish, although that too would change in the 1970s). The Ballet helped them raise a hitherto low self-esteem. They developed an appreciation of who and what they were and no longer felt a need to apologize or feel guilty about their heritage.

At the same time CYO youths maintained one foot in the world of Anglo America, a world that until 1961 had overshadowed their in-group experiences. Public education and the power of popular culture had acted subtly to acculturate these young people into the dominant culture; in fact, most of the dancers spoke English as their primary language.

The emphasis in the CYO remained on Americanization, moreover. Father Vincent, in his attempts to instill a further sense of pride among the CYO members, used the CYO to socialize the members to the world of middle-class decorum. By insisting on formally run meetings, Father Vincent taught CYO members parliamentary procedure and social skills that they normally would have never developed. Much of the membership descended from working-class backgrounds, and as high school students seldom participated in campus organization activities. The city's public high school population was divided by race and class while featuring a faculty and administration that were almost exclusively Anglo. The school prepared students to take on middle-class leadership positions, while teaching Mexican American students to find their proper place in society as workers.[40]

But Father Vincent's CYO opened the door to a new world for OLS's youth. In addition to mastering Robert's Rules of Order, CYO members also learned the value of democratic procedure, voting on important issues themselves rather than having Father Vincent or other adult leaders dictate policy and procedure to them. They learned how to organize campaigns so that upon attending state conventions they could elect some of their members to statewide CYO offices. The CYO in the 1960s and 1970s, therefore, offered Mexican American youths opportunities to discover both their roots in Mexican American culture and the skills needed to succeed in the future. Although Father Vincent's actions may be seen as empowering Mexican American Catholic youth in ways that might in the future allow them to level substantive challenges to an oppressive status quo, that was not the case. The CYO taught skills necessary for success within the existing social and political environment and so muted any chances for true radicalism among the group's members. Certainly, promoting pride in Mexican culture did not amount to teaching radical behavior.

By the 1980s Father Vincent had been transferred out of OLS. The CYO leadership then fell to the lay directorship of Patsy Hemmis who pushed the CYO toward involvement outside the parish. Hemmis remained faithful to Father Vincent's goal of instilling self-esteem (by teaching the students parliamentary procedure and allowing them to run their own affairs), but she emphasized duty to the community. First, she restructured the group. Hemmis developed a youth section for pre–high school dancers, mostly from the elementary grades. She had the entire Ballet attend mass once a month sporting vests: the younger members wore a caterpillar while the older members displayed a butterfly to symbolize, respectively, the unity between the two groups and a sense of shared destiny outside the immediate age cohort.[41] Further, Hemmis attempted to impress in her charges a deeply spiritual commitment to social responsibility in two other ways. Through various activities (among them attendance at mass) she strengthened the members' Catholic conviction. Prayers at the beginning and ending of meetings, and spiritual retreats, also reinforced civic obligation.[42]

Moreover, Hemmis encouraged the members to engage in community service such as regular visits to local nursing homes. But the most moving experience in the CYO, and with the most profound impact, came one Christmas (during the 1980s) when Hemmis asked members to go door to door (without reference to their organizational affiliation) throughout different sections across the city asking for food. Overall, the drive gathered food for the needy, but it had deeper effects. First, the young people experienced the hurt of heartless selfishness at Christmas time. Second, they felt the sting of racial prejudice. People slammed doors in their faces and issued a string of epithets. As they walked through middle-class Anglo neighborhoods, the youth were verbally assaulted and mocked. Hemmis's assignment proved extremely painful but it made the youngsters sensitive to the everyday lives of the less fortunate.[43]

Through the 1960s, 1970s, and 1980s the CYO remained working-class oriented. A substantial number of members, however, finished college and moved into the white-collar world. Even those CYO members who remained in Victoria's blue-collar neighborhoods took on new roles as adults in local community activities and political campaigns.

Over the course of three decades the CYO had brought Mexican American youths together and introduced them to their cultural heritage and taught them to embrace it and to take pride in it, though never advocating that members reject mainstream American popular culture. At the same time, the organization had exposed its followers to the procedures (and the cultural assumptions embedded in them) essential for success in the Anglo world. Finally, the CYO, under Hemmis's leadership, had made young people more aware of the hostile world in which they lived, and taught them to be sensitive to those less privileged. All the while these lessons emphasized (subtly or overtly) the correctness of basic American attitudes while discouraging militant or leftist challenges to the structural nature of American society. Democracy, the two party electoral system, free enterprise, and the traits of character and personal values that supposedly made them devoted workers were never brought into question. Like the other secular organizations of that age, however, the CYO offered its members a social/cultural space to define themselves as both Mexican and American.

Just as youths experienced satisfaction throughout the post–World War II years as members of the CYO, so too did adult parishioners find rewards in new religious movements. The 1960s saw some Catholics begin to seek alternative methods for expressing their faith and identity. For some churchgoers, the dogmatic emphasis by the Catholic faith on the need for official intermediaries (i.e., the priest and the sacraments) interfered with their ability to find a personal relationship with God. Such individuals found spiritual fulfillment in what is known as the Cursillo.

The Cursillo idea originated in Spain in 1949 when twenty-two laypersons climbed the mountainside to a monastery outside Palma de Mallorca and held a retreat. During the course of their weekend of self-examination, they developed a paradigm for generating renewed enthusiasm for their religious faith. From Spain this type of retreat spread across Western Europe. The movement came to the United States shortly thereafter through two Spanish Air Cadets stationed in Waco, Texas. From Central Texas, the movement quickly spread southward finding followers in San Antonio, the Rio Grande Valley, and points in between.[44]

The word "cursillo" means small course. Thus, the movement centers on the notion of holding a series of compact instructional lessons on Christianity so that laymen might be brought into closer contact with their faith. As a result of the new direction that the Cursillo movement offered Mexican American Catholics, hundreds of individuals (many of them previously uninvolved in church activities) attended Cursillo retreats and returned to their parishes with a burning zeal for the faith.[45] This spirit of enthusiasm found a niche in Our Lady of Sorrows Parish in 1961. Parishioners were attracted to the Cursillistas, as they were called, because the Cursillo experience was a deeply moving one that brought people in touch with the meaning of their faith at a level unattainable in mass or through reception of the sacraments.[46]

The clergy in general tolerated the Cursillo movement (a few priests even supported it strongly), but it caused dismay and even envy among pastors and fellow lay people who clung to a more traditional, circumscribed view of religiosity. The movement seemed to hold the seeds for disruption of the established Catholic order for several reasons. First, the sharing of prayer, exposure to skits, discussions, and other activities brought Catholic lay people into contact with their belief system on a deeper level than attainable heretofore.[47] The movement also emphasized the role of the laity in general and the individual specifically. Such premises stood in stark contrast to Catholic traditions of hierarchy and the need for clergy to interpret and properly explain the re-lationship of the individual to God. Interestingly enough, the doctrinal aspect of the Cursillo movement was based on a very traditional view of theology, the sacraments, and morality, even at the very time that Catholics were engaged in the reconsideration of Church teachings, structures, and institutions "that led to the Second Vatican Council."[48]

Also, different and appealing about the Cursillo movement (aside from its stress on lay participation and an existential emphasis) was its class-blindness. In other words, simply being a participant or be-ing moved to action by the spiritual experience was enough to allow one to assume a leadership role. Cursillismo opened up doors for self-expression to people other than the educated, the middle class or the clergy. Chicano historian Gilberto M. Hinojosa argues that Chican-ismo and Vatican II undercut the Cursillo movement and produced a steep decline in participation.[49] Such, however, was not the case in Victoria where it continued to thrive well after the 1960s.

One reason for this exception in Victoria is that Mexican Ameri-cans in the city have historically been careful about threats to the fun-damental assumptions of the existing order. Involvement in Cursillo ceremonialism maintained such a standard: participation allowed for the expression of a stronger sense of individuality among Victoria's Mexican American Catholics but within the parameters of traditional Catholic theology. It offered women in the organization the oppor-tunity to achieve a measure of spiritual equality with men without at-tempting to undermine their own authority in the home and work-place. It further offered parishioners the opportunity to explore their faith as individuals rather than as part of the flock. While the Cursillo idea posed an alternative to strict hierarchical practices it never advo-cated that Cursillistas leave the Church.[50]

Thus the Cursillo movement, as it unfolded in Victoria, supports one of Hinojosa's conclusions. He argues that the movement was

> a phenomenon that combined traditional *Mexicano* culture and spirituality with the post–World War II socialization pro-cesses Mexican Americans were undergoing. Urbanization and industrialization, accelerated in the forties and fifties by na-tional and international developments, disrupted the familial bond that held *Mexicano* communities together. Only a deep,

radical personal renewal could restore the efficacy of those bonds. And to that end the *Cursillo* movement emerged, advocating the restoration of the role of males in the family and in community.[51]

The Cursillos in Victoria, as did the Guadalupanas and the Ballet Folklorico, acted as an outlet wherein Mexican American Catholics could, in a particularly familiar place, create personal identities. Although potentially threatening to the Church (by encouraging a mass exodus to Protestantism) or to traditional values of male supremacy, the movement actually sought to offer adherents a new avenue for the expression of faith.

The early 1970s, meantime, was a period of deepening controversy within the OLS community. At the heart of matters was ongoing discontent with various priests. The first public evidence of such dissatisfaction arose in 1971 when Father Vincent Patrizi announced from the pulpit that he had received notice from the archbishop that an anonymous group within the congregation had written to ask for his removal. The letter allegedly criticized Patrizi, the pastor, for not being sensitive to the Mexican American community and failing to understand the "Mexican mentality."[52] Patrizi was incensed at such a charge. Given his ongoing work with the CYO and its Ballet Folklorico program, he believed that few non-Mexicans in Victoria better understood the Mexican people than he. And Patrizi had his defenders in the parish. Soila Rincón wrote a letter to Archbishop Francis Furey defending Patrizi and criticizing his assailants.[53] Many others sent in correspondence of support to Patrizi's superiors, but the majority of them were not OLS members. For example, one letter written in November of 1971 in support of Patrizi was signed by sixty-five individuals, only two of whom had Spanish surnames.[54]

The push to drive out Patrizi remained a shadowy affair with few parishioners openly stating their opposition to him. Calling for the priest's ouster was quite drastic for a community that had traditionally adhered to their faith in an acquiescent manner. As Catholics, parishioners held clergy in a place of honor, beyond reproach. The most vocal and visible of Patrizi's critics was Robert Álvarez, a local building contractor, who alleged insensitivity problems with the local priests. In November of 1971, Álvarez wrote to Archbishop Patrick Flores asking for the creation of a new Mexican American parish, noting that there were, at the time, three churches serving Anglos and that a new congregation with a priest who understood Mexicans seemed to be the only solution to existing disharmony.[55] For his part, Archbishop Flores argued that the majority of parishioners were happy with the priests and that "the Fathers in Victoria still have one of the best CCD [Confraternity of Christian Doctrine] projects in the diocese. They are interested in youth, as one can well see in the ballet which is the best in the States, and they are forever visiting patients, the aged, etc." [56] A new Mexican American parish was never created, and by 1972 Father Vincent Patrizi was reassigned to duties in Corpus Christi, Texas, ninety miles to the south. A former prison chaplain named Joseph Kelly took Patrizi's place.

This discord between Father Vincent Patrizi and a segment of the parishioners reflected growing tension between the Church (both locally and nationally) and the Mexican American community in the early 1970s. Mexican Americans never seriously challenged the institution in theological terms, but dissatisfaction with Patrizi's performance in Victoria did mirror a larger national trend of critical reexamination between Mexican Americans and the priesthood. Then events in the early 1980s brought the two back together in ways that seemed to bring hope for a measure of direct social action that had been previously lacking among Victoria's Mexican Americans.

The Catholic Church designated the Victoria area as a diocese in April of 1982, with David Grahmann the first archbishop. Grahmann sought to create an "authentic Church unifying a diverse people consisting of 16 ethnic groups." [57] But Grahmann attempted much more, having cut his ecclesiastical administrative teeth in San Antonio under the progressive thinking Robert E. Lucey. Archbishop Lucey, Grahmann's mentor, developed a reputation as a champion of social justice. Since his days as a priest he had used radio and the printed word to inform Catholics of the principles of social justice espoused by the popes through the encyclicals Rerum Novarum and Quadregsimo Ano, both of which argued for the right of workers to bargain collectively for just wages. He defended the cause of collective bargaining and in one instance, as bishop of the Archdiocese of Amarillo, he ordered that "all Church construction use union labor or at least pay union wages." Additionally, he argued that segregation was a sin.[58]

After Lucey's retirement, Grahmann remained in San Antonio and worked with subsequent archbishops Francis J. Fury and Patrick Flores. Through these years, Grahmann not only learned the administrative side of Catholicism, he also developed a deep respect for Mexican American culture and an awareness of Mexican American concerns.[59]

Thus even though Grahmann was originally from Hallettsville (forty-five miles northeast of Victoria) he brought to his new position none of the racist attitudes that were still prevalent in the Golden Crescent region, including Victoria. In pursuing an "authentic Church," therefore, Grahmann sought not lockstep conformity, nor homogeneity, but rather, to pursue a celebration of diversity and a machinery that could help liberate socially oppressed minority Catholics, especially Mexican Americans. Grahmann was interested in the struggle for equality regardless of whose feathers he ruffled. As OLS pastor David Colella put it: "On his radio program the bishop just comes right out and says: 'This is unjust and unfair.' He knows that those who have money will be angry, but he does not let such feelings come into the picture."[60]

Grahmann's interest in the working-class and Mexican American community went beyond the confines of church grounds and extended outside his office. In this vein he enlisted the assistance of Sisters Odelia Koreneck and Stephanie Marie Martínez to develop the Gulf Coast Organizing Effort (GCOE), a broad-based social action organization associated with the Industrial Areas Foundation (IAF), a social activist organization based on the Saul Alinsky model of protest.[61]

At first the GCOE began organizing cluster meetings of parishes in and around the Victoria area in attempts to drum up popular support and bring like-minded people together. While the idea was to draw in a wide array of local citizens, the majority of interested parties belonged to the Mexican American working class. Within two years Koreneck and Martínez had developed a sustained team that trained directly with the IAF and then began enlisting the cooperation of other non-Catholic churches, going so far as to establish an office in a shopping strip in the central part of the city.[62]

Koreneck and Martínez found that while people were concerned about community and family issues and social inequality, a general lack of higher education and experience in confronting authority figures in the community meshed with a traditional air of intimidation to hinder execution of assignments. One of the more important actions by the GCOE then was to conduct what were called "one-on-ones," in which select individual members would be shown how to contact community political and economic leaders. The person would then go with one of the sisters to meet the targeted leader to discuss in general and unassuming terms specific problems that the individual had the power to address.[63]

In 1989 the GCOE succeeded in drawing members from Victoria and five surrounding counties to Our Lady of Sorrows' CCD Center for a special delegate assembly. This was the high point for the GCOE for a number of reasons. First, it had succeeded in attracting a heterogeneous group of speakers and audience members from the Anglo-, African, and Mexican American communities. Second, the meeting also involved a cross-section of various denominations that came from both middle- and working-class backgrounds. Finally, and perhaps most significantly, many of the speakers were rank-and-file members who had been groomed over the years to take leadership roles within the movement.[64]

Unfortunately, the organization engaged in little work during the 1990s. The Church moved Bishop Grahmann to Dallas and the two sisters to a troubled Catholic school in San Antonio's predominantly Mexican American west side. The timing of these moves appears suspicious, but there is no documentation to indicate some larger conspiracy. Sisters Odelia and Marie have not articulated suspicions about the timing of the moves. Thus, the removal of the GCOE core leadership and the subsequent demise of the organization may have been the result of an unfortunate coincidence.

FOR A TIME, early in the century, the Church often reflected the broader bigotry of the larger society. Notwithstanding those attitudes Mexican Americans continually used the church as a nurturing center for their culture (as with the Guadalupanas and the Cursillo movement), as a vehicle for the expression of their patriotism (as with the CWV), as a training ground for the development of skills necessary to function within Anglo society (as with the CYO), and as a learning environment for realizing social awareness and the value of civic action (as with the CYO under Hemmis and the short-lived GCOE). Mexican Americans used the church as a center for cultural preservation, community empowerment, and citizenship making.

Yet Mexican American church organizations, much as secular organizations, never questioned the fundamental suppositions of American society. Instead, they stressed the acceptance of hegemonic American values such as Christianity, social order, and patriotism. Such groups promoted parliamentary procedure, participatory democracy, and personal responsibility, the very types of practices at the heart of American citizenship. In short, the church organizations in the city became a bulwark against extreme ideologies. Comparatively, Mexican American Catholics in other locations, like Houston, Texas, used the church to question mainstream institutions.[65]

Church organizations in Victoria muted a deeper critique of the society to which their Mexican American parishioners belonged. Mexican Americans understood differences in wealth and status within the parish, for instance, but they did not view these as the results of some type of larger inequitable socioeconomic force. Within the various church organizations, in fact, the membership disclosed little awareness of class differences existing within the church ranks. Only within the GCOE was there ever any chance for class-consciousness to surface as an issue, but given the brevity of the GCOE's life activists never had the opportunity to explore such complexities.

Overall, Catholic church groups adopted, albeit in somewhat tempered form, the dominant ideology that informed widespread definitions of Americanism. As such, Victoria's Mexican American Catholics defined themselves as Mexican and as American in ways that seemed practical, but which did not voice any serious disapproval or challenge to the structural status quo. They simply sought to act to bring about a more equitable society within extant social, economic, and political parameters.

3
Creating Loyal Citizens

The Relationship between Mexican Americans
and the Victoria Independent School District

T HE MEXICAN AMERICANS' identity in Victoria was shaped
partly by experiences with the Victoria public schools. Originally excluded from the school system, later included but
segregated, and finally nominally integrated, Mexican American students found that the schools existed not just to enlighten young people
and promote an egalitarian society but to reflect and reproduce existing
social norms as well, among them those that dictated segregation based
on the perceived racial inferiority of Mexicans. Generally speaking,
Mexican Americans differentiated between these two cross-purposes.
When they questioned the school system, especially in the second half
of the twentieth century, they never voiced a critique of the fundamental values promoted in the public school curriculum. Instead, they
challenged the discriminatory nature of the school district as an im-
pediment to their children's abilities to take part in economic and political competition on an even footing.

Until the 1960s the Victoria public school system practiced de facto
segregation and followed the prescription that every child receiving
public schooling ought to become Americanized. Segregation arose out
of the social order imposed after the Texas Revolution, and even though
nominal integration began during the years of World War I, most children attended separate schools for years after. The era of nominal integration (circa 1917 to the mid-1960s) was marked by the aforementioned

belief that the entire student body should be homogeneous; thus, widely accepted Anglo ideals should be inculcated upon Mexican American students. But despite integration, school personnel treated Mexican American youngsters as second-class citizens. As institutions, therefore, the public schools contributed to a larger social process that promoted a type of dual reality. True that the public school curriculum promoted the principle that all citizens were equal and thus had ready access to power, but at the same time another truth — public segregation, discrimination, and disenfranchisement — taught very different lessons to Mexican American school children and their families. Segregated from the beginning Victoria's public schools remained much the same way after the 1954 *Brown v. Board of Education* decision. Mexican American children dealt with racist teachers and administrators, while Mexican American professionals experienced employment discrimination. For most of the twentieth century the political structure excluded Mexican American adults from fair representation on the school board by maintaining an at-large electoral structure that benefited Anglo candidates. These actualities undermined the dominant culture's attempt to legitimize a benign social order.

The practice of establishing public schools specifically for Mexican Americans began in 1902 in Seguin, Texas. The example of the Seguin school system soon spread, especially throughout the southern part of the state, so that by 1930 South Texas maintained separate school facilities for Mexicans wanting an education. School segregation dovetailed with existing social practices: Anglo-Americans could not allow the paradox of maintaining a segregated, stratified social order while allowing Mexican Americans equal educational opportunities in the same facilities as Anglos.[1] Further, in the eyes of Anglo leaders, a limited education for Mexican Americans posed no threat since Mexicans were not to be permitted a level of education or economic attainment that could seriously overturn public opinion or policy. Moreover, school segregation served the vested interest of those at the top, for it helped maintain a pliable labor force. The unstated goal of officials around the state, including Victoria, was to ensure the continuance of a hierarchical society wherein people of color acted as a proletariat. Tapping into a pool of illiterate workers could best bring this about.

Anglo society believed that Mexican Americans had little or no interest in education. The thinking of the period held that the intelligence, perseverance, and the work ethic necessary for success — and therefore essential to full citizenship — were inherent to the white race; intellectually inferior Mexicans lacked any such set of values.[2] When white officials extended schooling to Mexicans, motives other than democratic ideals dictated policy and curriculum. Gilbert Gonzalez, who examined the educational experiences of Mexican Americans in the Southwest during the first half of the twentieth century, sees the educational system in the United States as having served the needs of a capitalist economy.[3] Similarly, Anglo employers in Texas, particularly those who made their livelihood from agriculture, feared that an equal (and quality) education would draw Mexican labor away from the low paying field jobs to which they had been relegated.[4] It was general knowledge throughout the state that the "Mexican schools" were hardly adequate to prepare students for anything other than manual work, thus employers hardly resisted a dual school system such as the one they financed through their tax contributions. In Victoria, segregation automatically ensured the continuation of an uneducated underclass of Mexicans Americans as elsewhere.

School segregation also served to remind those involved of their standing in the social order. Lower-class Anglos particularly resisted integration because they feared any changes that might imply a measure of equality between Mexicans and Anglos could lead to increased job competition. Just as poor southern whites expected deference from blacks and supported a racially based social hierarchy, so too did working-class Texans endorse school separation for it reassured them, at least superficially, of their status as superiors over people of color.[5]

Separate schools further acted to reconcile the reality of a segregated social order with egalitarian principles fundamental to the American political tradition for which American blood had been shed. White elites showed little interest in promoting a truly equal society, and so school district officials engaged in discriminatory hiring practices, thereby bringing the racially segregated, privileged society it served into the structure of the district. The overwhelming white nature of school districts' (including the Victoria Independent School District) faculty and administrative staff served as a symbol of Anglo political and social hegemony. But the structure of the school system collided with the ideals of equality and republicanism taught in the classroom. Segregated schooling distinguished for impressionable youngsters the difference between civics lessons and the reality of everyday experience.[6] Segregation reinforced the nature of the dominant culture's limited definition of citizenship, a definition that withheld the most prized privileges and opportunities for whites.

The larger project of the segregated public schools was the creation not only of educated citizens but also of patriotic ones who could sustain and defend a capitalist democratic republic and fight against radical doctrines without question. To accomplish this, the schools attempted to create a sense of shared experience and shared fate among all students. Mexican American children were targeted for assimilation by a curriculum that centered largely on English acquisition and values inculcation. A homogenized society might be realized if foreigners were brought into line by exposure to superior white values and culture. Indeed, those at the top of the Texas state educational administration voiced such desires. State Superintendent of Schools Annie Webb Blanton cited the experience of World War I as having shown in dramatic relief the need for Americanization. She pointed to the 1910 census that showed 13 million foreign-born Americans who spoke fifty-four languages. Moreover, she noted that in Texas alone, with a population of 3.8 million, there were 241,938 foreign born, over 67,000 of whom were illiterate and that one-fourth of the men examined for military service during the war "could not read a newspaper or write a letter home." Thus for Blanton, illiteracy, ignorance, and the specter of un-Americanism went hand in hand. Education, in her view, could combat both types of social ills. The public schools should serve, therefore, not only to teach but also to provide the ideological heat to warm "the melting pot of America."[7]

What was the impact of segregationist thinking on Mexican Americans? Obviously, it hardly equipped youngsters for competition in the marketplace. Lower levels of spending per pupil, poor physical plants, and a default vocational track system victimized them and took a toll.[8] Further, a segregationist mentality denied Mexican Americans deserved educational opportunity since society hardly regarded instruction for Mexicans as an absolute commitment. Because the majority of Mexican Americans prior to 1940 lived in rural areas they seldom had access to schooling.[9] Poverty stricken, they worked together in family groups anonymous to school officials who had little consideration for their uplifting anyway. Even when drawn into the educational network,

Mexican American students experienced less than a satisfactory response to their interests, encountering teachers who were either indifferent or inadequate.[10]

THE POLICY of segregation placed Mexican Americans in an ambivalent relationship with the schools. In the classroom Mexican Americans learned two sets of contradictory lessons. On the one hand, daily experiences with Anglo teachers and administrators taught them that they were poorer, culturally disadvantaged, and inferior. But on the other hand their classroom lessons also emphasized the concepts of freedom and equality.[11] Blanton's goals of encouraging assimilation and promoting civic-mindedness and patriotism, therefore, acted as a double-edged sword. Mexican American children accepted the dominant culture's emphasis on a widely understood set of ideals that reified such goals as social harmony, egalitarianism, patriotism, the work ethic, and Christianity. But these same values led Mexican Americans to question a segregated, racist order that contrasted with the lessons of "Americans all." Youngsters saw themselves as American citizens deserving of first-class treatment. They looked upon the vote, public office, and access to the courts as a birthright. Thus did a school system that emphasized accommodation engender the sense that protest served on its own as a lever for challenging inequality.

As many Mexican Americans took these teachings to heart, they sincerely trusted that education held the potential to bring about a more egalitarian society. Education would allow their children and grandchildren to work their way out of poorly paid manual labor and into white-collar professional positions. The attendant status that followed the rise of a professional class, so it was believed, could empower future generations of American leaders to contribute to the creation of a more just social order for Mexican Americans.

It was the inspiration of such egalitarian ideas that moved Victoria's Mexican American population toward action for a color-blind school system. To be sure, such steps were never confrontational. First of all, working-class Mexican Americans lacked the influence and experience to challenge the school system. Many also feared retribution by Anglo employers. There was too much to be lost by rocking the educational boat for members of the middle class who needed the support of local Anglo bankers, businessmen, and politicians for their economic sur-

This photo of the Charles A. Leuschner home was taken ca. 1890. Leuschner later rented the home to the school district for use as a "Mexican school." *Courtesy Victoria Regional History Center, Victoria College/UH-Victoria Library*

vival. To be denied a needed loan, a building permit, the informal support of other businessmen, or a friendly ear in city hall if an exception to local ordinances was needed could be inconvenient at least and devastating at worst. Yet if they trod carefully, self-employed business owners did have more freedom to undertake subtle challenges to educational discrimination.

The earliest challenge to the Victoria school system came in 1916 at the hand of Carlos Delgado, a recently arrived immigrant from Mexico, who learned of the inferior conditions encountered by Mexican American students in the Victoria public schools. Unlike other Mexican Americans in Victoria County, he was not employed by an Anglo ranch, farm, or business owner. Rather he had his own business and depended not only Anglo clientele but rather on other Mexican Americans in the community. Thus Delgado had greater leeway to stand up to injustice as he was not subject to the immediate consequences others faced.[12]

Delgado sought the best education possible for his children and took steps to gain access to the white schools for his Texas-born offspring. He asked the pastor of the Mexican Presbyterian Church, Reverend Cayetano Acevedo, for assistance. The two men convinced a local Anglo businessman, who remained anonymous, to help them acquire equal educational opportunities for Mexican American children. Together Delgado, Acevedo, and the anonymous Anglo businessman wrote a petition that Delgado then presented to the board in the name of "all Mexican Americans in Victoria" (actually few of his countrymen volunteered to sign the complaint, fearing retribution by Anglo employers). The text contained nothing that may be considered accusative, insubordinate, or impertinent; instead its content centered on the need for a proper education as the vehicle to create productive citizens:

> To deny integration for the Mexican-American's child imposes a lifetime hardship on a discrete class of children not held accountable for their disabling status. The stigma of illiteracy, through the lack of proper teachers, will mark them for the rest of their lives.
>
> By denying these children a basic education, we deny them the ability to live within the structure of our civic institutions, and foreclose any realistic possibility that they will contribute in even the smallest way to the program of our nation. And, whenever our nation calls upon them to serve this country, they will not be able to give full service capabilities.[13]

Given the national zeitgeist in 1916 that was strongly influenced by the world war, such an unthreatening appeal—based on the desire to have the schools shape citizens fully capable of serving their country in time of need—likely held more sway than it would have during peacetime.

Whether the board was moved by wartime concerns, the persuasive rhetoric of the petition, or the influence of the anonymous benefactor, Mexican American children, including Carlos Delgado's two oldest sons, began attending public schools with white students in 1917. The Delgado siblings' daily interaction with Anglo students and teachers was at times difficult, thereby foreshadowing the experience other Mexican American pupils would face later in the century as schools in Texas, California, and other states were forced to integrate.[14]

Thus does Victoria's educational history provide the first example of a Texas school district closing a Mexican school for the purposes of integration in the twentieth century. Nowhere else in Texas did Mexicans manage to do away with the Mexican schools this early. But it was not a permanent concession. Three years after the end of the war there was an attempt in the city to reestablish a separate educational facility for Mexican American students.[15] This issue, however, ended in compromise as Victoria opted for a policy of nominal integration instead. The school board decided at a meeting held in October of 1920 against total segregation, but with reservations. Whether to soothe the fears of Anglos or because it believed such measures were necessary, the board, at the same meeting, stated that students with vermin or contagious diseases of any kind were to be sent home. Such a disclaimer was likely necessary because Anglo parents feared mixing their children with "dirty" Mexican students whose very character, in the white mind, had been marked as unclean.[16] The wording of the board's decision reveals how men in power perceived (and acted as a consequence) Mexican American students: foreigners likely to be unhygienic. Nowhere in the board's pronouncement are Mexican American children referred to as citizens, rather they are only called "Mexicans."[17]

NOMINAL INTEGRATION in the Victoria public school system persisted until around 1964. It was during the 1960s that Mexican Americans individually and collectively took a more active (albeit an accommodationist and consensual) role in combating discrimination in the public schools. In so doing, they followed the lead of civic organizations such as LULAC and the AGIF, which had organized (in 1929 and 1948, respectively) to fight for Mexican American inclusion into mainstream American life and for equal access to education.[18]

LULAC mounted the first legal challenge to segregated education in 1946 when it supported the American Civil Liberties Union in its representation of Gonzalo Méndez and other Mexican Americans in Southern California who argued that the segregated schools their children attended were unconstitutional. The U.S. District Court in San Diego found that such practices were indeed a violation of the Fourteenth Amendment of the U.S. Constitution. The court acknowledged the reasonableness of pedagogical arguments for separation of Spanish speaking children at early ages. But such a position, the court argued, did not justify segregation into the middle-school years and beyond. Taking a cue from the California decision, on April 8, 1947, Price Daniel, the Texas attorney general, issued an opinion stating that Mexican American children could not be discriminated against solely on the basis of race. He did allow that Mexican American students who suffered serious language deficiencies could be put in separate classrooms, or even different schools in order to facilitate their learning of the English language, but only as far as the third grade.

The following January the Texas LULAC assisted Mexican American parents in filing suit against the Bastrop Independent School District (BISD). Later joined by the AGIF, LULAC succeeded in persuading the United States District Court that segregation was a violation of the Fourteenth Amendment. Federal judge Ben Rice found that segregation on the basis of ethnicity was discriminatory and unconstitutional. He further ordered the BISD to integrate within one year. He agreed with the finding in California that permitted segregation due to language difficulties, but ordered that such segregation could only take place after scientific testing was administered to all students, Mexican American and white, and that such segregation could not take place after the first grade. Other Texas school districts either ignored the ruling or schemed to circumvent it, however. In 1957 San Antonio lawyers Gus García and James De Anda, with LULAC support, sued the Driscoll school district accusing it of not giving scientifically developed, standardized tests to all students. Rather it practiced systematic separation of Mexican children, on the basis of race, by separating them into different classes in the first and second grades. The federal court agreed with García and De Anda that such a policy clearly violated the Fourteenth Amendment. Such cases helped pave the way for inclusion of Mexican American children in previously all-white public schools in Texas and set the backdrop to what would unfold in Victoria by the next decade.[19]

At midcentury the separate Mexican school in Victoria had been abandoned for over thirty-three years and Mexican American children had at least been nominally integrated into the white public school system. But the situation was different for African American students in the city. Since everyone could remember, the VISD maintained a separate facility for black students, and it remained adamant on black/white segregation long after *Brown v. Board of Education* (1954). Although this chapter focuses on the experience of Mexican Americans, a brief look at the school district's response to the *Brown* decision is instructive, for the Anglo dominated school system followed a pattern of resistance and foot dragging toward governmentally mandated change that lasted through the next five decades. This tactic set the tone for an increasingly antagonistic stand against Mexican Americans who would, with the assistance of the federal government (which many local Anglos resented), lobby for better education in the modern era.

In August of 1955 the VISD Board met and argued (in response to the *Brown* decision of the previous year) that it would be impossible to integrate African American students by the 1955–56 school year due to shortages of classroom space at all grade levels. The school board employed a tone of benevolent paternalism in its argument against immediate integration claiming that "any integration at the present time would jeopardize the educational opportunities of all students." Members of the board went on record as saying, "The Victoria School Board feels that its primary responsibility is to see that the school system is operated in the best interests of all school children." [20] Despite such seemingly benign reasoning, the board continued to outline separate budget allotments for black and white schools rather than actively seeking ways to integrate more quickly. Moreover, it also continued to spend $9 on white students for every $1 spent on black students. [21] Perhaps school board members hoped, as did their counterparts in other school districts across the South, that someone would ultimately figure out a way around integration. In postponing the inevitable, the board argued that "any integration at the present time would jeopardize the educational opportunities of all students." [22]

Nonetheless, on April 16, 1956, the board, after meeting with black and white members of the community, developed a plan for integrating children from the separate African American school into the district at large. Grades one through three were to abide by the new directive during the 1956–57 school year. All African American children who wished to attend other schools during the coming school year were to register at the separate black school, F. W. Gross, during the week of April 23–27. Unless students applied for a transfer from Gross School with their parents' signature, they would be required to spend the 1956–57 school year at Gross.[23] On February 3, 1958, a school board motion carried permitting black children to attend white schools through the sixth grade beginning in September 1958.[24] By 1960 the entire school district had been integrated, at least nominally. Separately identified "black" or "Mexican" schools had finally disappeared. But neighborhoods remained generally segregated and so did the schools therein. Despite efforts at integration the district still abided by discriminatory policies and practices. This posture would lead to increased discontent by Mexican Americans.

The last third of the century, therefore, witnessed a steady challenge to the status quo. During this period Mexican Americans in Victoria developed a strategy of protest that centered on the goal of expanding the definition of citizenship in attempts to forge a more inclusive society. In their minds citizenship meant Mexican American equality with Anglos in American society. Victoria's Mexican Americans felt they had proven their loyalty and patriotism in World Wars I and II. Like other Americans, they had pursued higher education in order to improve their qualifications as better citizens. Furthermore, Victoria's Mexican Americans had consciously shunned radicalism of any sort. Such behaviors, they contended, offered ample evidence that they had, as American society expected them to, internalized the traits inculcated upon them by the schools, the media, the churches, and every other mainstream institution. In short, Mexican Americans in Victoria believed themselves worthy to push ahead and shape a social order that no longer regarded them as a marginal people.

Until 1958 no minority candidate had successfully managed to break the color bar of the VISD School Board. The first to do so was attorney Manuel Velasco, who successfully ran for a school board position that year by focusing on his professional status and avoiding ethnic considerations. As will be argued in chapter 5, such early political hopefuls were forced to promote themselves as mainstream candidates who transcended racial or ethnic concerns.

During his single term on the board Velasco focused primarily on issues directly related to the functioning of the district as a unit rather than on ones of inequality and discrimination.[25] For Velasco, election (particularly within an at-large voting system) was a victory in itself. Thus his primary responsibility was to prove himself as a contributing, responsible member of the board. In this way, he could promote the notion that responsibility and integrity were not solely Anglo characteristics. Despite his single term on the board, Victoria voters were not prepared to make Mexican American presence a permanent feature of their school board. It would be four years after Velasco's tenure before another Mexican American could gain access to the board.

The second Mexican American to run successfully for the school board was John Artero, the owner of a local mortuary, who was elected in 1964 and served a single term until 1967. Artero's electoral success stemmed from the racialist nature of voting habits in Victoria. He was the only Mexican American candidate running for his place on the school board against three Anglos. Artero won the Mexican American vote, and a small measure of the white vote. Because of the large number of Anglo-American candidates in the race, however, white voters cancelled one another's votes in a three way split leaving Artero the victor. In the four-man race Victorians cast 2,693 votes. Artero received 833 of these, meaning that the other three candidates split the remaining 1,860 votes fairly closely and thus permitted Artero to win a plurality. A closer examination of the returns shows that Artero won decisively in areas that had a significant percentage of Mexican American voters and was defeated in wards populated predominantly by Anglo-Americans.[26]

Hopkins School and the courthouse, where Artero had significant majorities, were both located on the south side of the city and were heavily populated by Mexican Americans. The closeness of the race at the Patti Welder Junior High School was a function of the school's locality on the southeastern part of Victoria, which, though it maintained a sizable Anglo population, was by this time in the process of becoming predominantly Mexican American. As to the central portion of the city (as represented by the voting at Crain Junior High School), Mexican Americans in 1964 were just beginning to populate the neighborhood. Artero thus received more votes in this area than in any other part of Victoria, but he still came in last in total votes. Smith school was situated on the city's north side and so the results accurately reflected the predominance of the white middle class that supported the three white candidates. Finally, Wood and Guadalupe were both rural

Table 1. Vote by Boxes in 1964 School Board Election: Place Five.

Voting Place	Artero	H. W. Kacy	T. A. Jones	Thomas Tighe
Hopkins School	241	11	17	8
Courthouse	124	64	54	24
Crain Jr. High	273	325	383	348
Patti Welder Jr. High	91	91	80	69
Smith School	59	109	79	122
Guadalupe School	32	14	13	7
Wood School	10	5	4	4
Absentee	3	5	16	8
Totals	833	624	646	590

Source: *Victoria Advocate*, Victoria, Texas, April 5, 1964.

schools. Traditionally, the rural boxes were dominated by higher white voter turnout.

Artero was succeeded by Martín Cano, owner of an electrical supply store, who held office from the early 1970s through the early 1980s. Cano's long tenure indicated a tacit acceptance of a permanent Mexican American seat on the board. Until the creation of single-member districts, however, the presence of a Mexican American on the school board was contingent upon the candidate's appearance as accommodative to the status quo.

The Mexican American campaign for better education in the city took a marked turn in the 1970s when the department of Health, Education and Welfare (HEW) began investigating the VISD for possible violations of Title VI of the Civil Rights Act of 1964. Despite the fact that the U.S. Supreme Court outlawed racial segregation in 1954, and that Mexican Americans began to make inroads in terms of their ability to get elected to the school board, the VISD still imposed segregation under the guise of neighborhood schools and continued to discriminate in its employment practices. Such transgressions brought federal intervention at the request of Mexican Americans.

The last three decades of the century witnessed the increasing use of the judicial system by Mexican Americans to challenge long-standing violations of students' rights. This initiative took the form of lawsuits against the school district in efforts to gain access to fair employment opportunities, to replace the discriminatory at-large voting system with a single-member district system, and to challenge illegal actions by the school board. This series of lawsuits represented a new dimension in the manner Mexican Americans had come to see themselves. As first-class citizens deserving of full equality, they had in the federal government a potentially powerful ally to overturn historical wrongs.

Federal assistance, according to this logic, would be crucial to reaching an educational status that in turn meant improved career opportunities in the professions. A new generation of Mexican American professionals could well enhance the status of the community and validate any Mexican American critique of the social order. Equal citizens acting in the capacity of professionals could lead the charge for seeking the overall material improvement of the Mexican American community.

School district officials decided to fight federal fire with federal fire by contacting Texas senator Lloyd Bentsen and asking him to intervene on the district's behalf. In August, 1971, district superintendent C. O. Chandler had not yet received an answer from HEW on the district's proposed blueprint for ethnic balancing. What Chandler did receive that month was a reply from Bentsen stating that he had urged HEW and Richard Nixon to accept VISD's recommendations.[27]

The district proposed a plan to close down several south side, predominantly minority, schools and bus those children across town to mainly white schools. The problem was that under this arrangement only minority children suffered disruptions in their daily routines. Concerned parents such as Emelie P. Montelongo addressed the board in September, 1971, and complained about the one-sided nature of the board's decision. Board member Lee Allbright responded by saying that the only other alternative was to close down the schools anyway but not offer district buses to get minority children across town. The implication of his statement was that there existed no chance of north side schools closing down, or of busing white children to the south side.[28] In the end no busing was ever enforced, but HEW continued to monitor developments in the VISD.

By the fall of 1975 Superintendent C. O. Chandler had retired and the district had replaced him with Roger Gee. In reaction to HEW's persistent oversight of the district, Gee insisted that, "We don't think we're doing anything wrong." But while the district's minority enrollment as a whole was just under 35 percent, three of the schools named in the investigation action had minority enrollment of over 95 percent, and two others had minority enrollment of 83 percent.[29] The superintendent's strategy of embracing the concept of neighborhood schools had the benefit of appealing to all parents, none of whom wanted their children to be bused across town, while simultaneously maintaining a strong measure of de facto segregation.

Indeed members of the minority community held mixed feelings concerning the ongoing investigations initiated by HEW. Some minority residents saw the HEW action as potentially detrimental due to the likelihood of seeing busing become the means to achieve racial balance. Others saw any action to end a segregated school system as a positive step. In December of 1975, C. R. Callis, a local African American businessman and community leader, wrote to the *Victoria Advocate*: "I don't think HEW should dictate to us or order us around. I have talked to a lots of taxpayers, parents, and other citizens, and about 99 per cent are for neighborhood schools."[30] Callis went on to argue against the possibility of closing some neighborhood schools by forcing integration through busing. By contrast, Beatrice Flores argued in the *Victoria Advocate* that the HEW action was a welcome sign of change and that it was high time for discrimination in the public schools to end: "Anytime a case of this nature is brought before a judge, it is a victory in itself. Would this have been possible ten years ago? Discrimination in our schools is a fact. I should know. I grew up with it, and now my children are growing up with it; only now we don't have to put up with it. Thanks to HEW."[31]

Flores's open welcome of the federal government reflected a growing sense, among Mexican Americans, of their power as American citizens. And in fact the 1971 HEW suit was followed by a series of other legal complaints filed by Mexican Americans throughout the 1970s and 1980s. In the federal government, Mexican Americans had found an ally in the attempt to advance their rights.

As the dispute over busing and integration unfurled, Mexican Americans in Victoria turned to another pertinent issue: the lack of

**Table 2. Enrollment by Race and Ethnicity in Six VISD
Schools Named in HEW Investigation.**

School	Mexican American	Black	White	Total Number of Students
Dudley	68.1%	27.2%	4.7%	169
Gross	74.9%	23.9%	1.2%	259
Hopkins	72%	24.8%	3.2%	403
Juan Linn	69.9%	14.1%	15.9%	427
Mitchell	75.1%	12.2%	11.0%	237

Source: "VISD Threatened with State Action," *Victoria Advocate*, Oct. 31, 1975.

Mexican American role models in the schools. The VISD had as late
as the 1970s failed to create equal employment opportunities for minority teachers, thus depriving students of individuals identifiable with
their unique experiences and perspectives. The school board had hired
a few Spanish surnamed teachers as far back as the early part of the century to teach in the Mexican school, but as of 1960, out of the district's
314 teachers, only seven had Spanish surnames.[32]

The question of fair hiring practices arose in the tension-filled atmosphere of the early 1970s. Director of personnel Harry Uthoff in
April 1973 explained the matter of a Hispanic teacher shortage by noting the district lost about the same number of minority teachers every
year as it gained and that state competition was keen for recruitment of
bilingual specialists.[33] There was no mention of how the district might
take a more proactive role and aggressively recruit minority teachers for
the district.

On August 16, 1973, Uthoff informed the board that he had employed eighty-five new faculty, fourteen of whom were Mexican American and four of whom were African American. He went on to say that
he had interviewed fourteen more Mexican Americans, ten of whom
declined to work for the district, and four of whom originally agreed
to come to VISD but reneged before school started.[34] At this time minority students comprised 44.78 percent of the district's enrollment,
whereas the figures cited by Uthoff reflected a minority presence of
only 18.82 percent among all district teachers.

Fourteen months later Superintendent Gee and Uthoff addressed the school board and said that the district was still making a concerted effort to hire more minority instructors. Uthoff claimed to have no "exact figure" for the number of minority group teachers in the district but he estimated the number to be around 20 percent.[35]

The low percentage of minority teachers in VISD also concerned HEW officials. During HEW hearings in 1976 Harry Uthoff testified that since 1972 minority hiring of professional staff had increased by 98 percent whereas the district had only hired two Anglo-Americans. Moreover, he argued that of the district's 723 professional staff, approximately 15 percent were minority, which was about average for the state as a whole.[36] But the veracity of Uthoff's figures was successfully challenged in a lawsuit then underway involving Cristobal García.

In 1970 García, a VISD teacher, received his state certification for counseling. He then sought promotion to the position of counselor in VISD three times over the next five years. The board turned him down on each occasion. Realizing that his lack of success had less to do with the needs of the district or his qualifications than with the color of his skin, García first complained to the Equal Employment Opportunity Commission (EEOC). After reviewing his case the EEOC suggested that García had sufficient grounds to file a lawsuit against the school district. In April of 1977 a federal judge agreed to hear García's case as a class action suit on behalf of other Mexican Americans who might have experienced similar discrimination at the hands of the VISD in the past.[37]

Lawyers for García and other members of the class deluged the court on August 15, 1977, with a flood of statistics gathered from the school district and the Texas Education Agency. Plaintiff lawyers argued that of the district's professional faculty for the 1975–76 school year only 5.8 percent were Mexican American, whereas the district's enrollment was 35.4 percent Mexican American. The ratio of white students to white teachers was 11 to 1, but for African Americans the ratio was 23 to 1, and for Mexican Americans it was 73 to 1. The statewide ratio of Mexican American teachers to Mexican American students in the 1972–73 school year had been 71 to 1, but in VISD the ratio had been 170 to 1. Moreover, these lawyers argued, the median income for teachers in VISD was $8,031, yet only 2.2 percent of Mexican American educators earned a figure above the median.[38] In related testimony given during the previous HEW hearings in 1973, however, personnel director Harry Uthoff had argued that the district maintained between 15 to 20 percent minority faculty, and plaintiff lawyers now presented these data in the Cristobal García case.

How did Uthoff arrive at such disparate figures? There are three possible answers that together account for the differences. First, Uthoff may have spoken of minority faculty that would have included African Americans and presumably Asian Americans or other teachers who were not white. Second, as disclosed during the course of the García trial, the district had classified Mexican American women who were married to Anglos as Mexican American, while listing white women married to Mexican American men as Mexican American also, thus boosting the apparent number of Mexican Americans on the district's payroll.[39] Finally, it is possible that, intentionally or not, Uthoff may have presented inflated figures during HEW investigations as he often spoke in generalities giving rounded percentages rather than concrete terms. Regardless, the judge accepted the data offered by the plaintiff lawyers and not Uthoff's.

In fact Uthoff's and the district's credibility had been severely compromised early in the proceedings. Judge Cox noted that:

> The history of Defendants' reluctance to cooperate with discovery began at the inception of this suit. In response to Plaintiffs' interrogatories, Defendants gave an evasive response that all of the information sought was contained in the records of the District. Yet, after the Court ordered those records opened after Plaintiffs filed a motion to compel, the Defendants refused access to those records. It was only after Plaintiffs filed a second motion to compel that Defendants cooperated.[40]

Plaintiff lawyers for García persuasively argued that the VISD had indeed maintained a tradition of discrimination against Mexican Americans in its employment practices. Not only had the district sustained a poor record of hiring Mexican Americans in proportion to the percentage of Mexican American students enrolled in the VISD but it had also failed to promote Mexican Americans. Although the percentage of Spanish-surnamed educators in the district increased between the 1972–73 and the 1976–77 school years from 4.23 percent to 8.3 percent, the region of South Texas had shown an upswing of Mexican

Table 3. Ratio of Spanish-Surnamed Students to Spanish-Surnamed Teachers in VISD, 1967–77.

Year	% Spanish-Surnamed Students	% Spanish-Surnamed Educators
1967–68	28.9	2.69
1968–69	33.5	4.26
1969–70	34.3	3.81
1970–71	34.5	4.41
1971–72	34.9	4.49
1972–73	35.9	4.23
1973–74	35.0	4.97
1974–75	35.4	5.89
1975–76	36.8	8.51
1976–77	36.6	8.30

Source: Court Order in The District Court of the United States for the Southern District of Texas, Victoria Division, July 24, 1978, 3.

Table 4. Percentage of Mexican American Educators in Victoria and the State, 1972–77.

Year	% MA Educators in Victoria*	% MA Educators in South Texas
1972–73	4.2	17.4
1973–74	5.0	19.2
1974–75	5.9	20.4
1975–76	8.5	22.0
1976–77	8.3	23.1

* "MA" stands for Mexican American

Source: Court Order in the District Court of the United States for the Southern District of Texas, Victoria Division, July 24, 1978, 4.

Table 5. Student to Teacher Ratios in School Districts Surrounding Victoria.

City	Ratio of Mexican American Teachers to Students
Kingsville	20:1
Alice	26:1
Corpus Christi	41:1
Victoria	73:1

Source: Court Order in the District Court of the United States for the Southern District of Texas, Victoria Division, July 24, 1978, 4.

Table 6. Promotions in VISD from 1969 to 1977 by Ethnicity.

Year	Number of Promotions	Mexican American Promotions*
1969	7	0.0
1970	6	0.0
1971	9	11.1
1972	6	0.0
1973–74	5	20.0
1974–75	11	9.0
1975–76	6	0.0
1976–77	3	0.0

* as a percentage of all promotions.

Source: Court Order in the District Court of the United States for the Southern District of Texas, Victoria Division, July 24, 1978, 5.

American educators from 17.4 percent to 23.1 percent during that same time. Moreover, Mexican Americans had received a minuscule number of promotions within the district from 1969 to 1977.

For the area of South Texas, the following figures showed that Victoria did indeed discriminate more than surrounding areas.

To further buttress their case, plaintiff lawyers brought out the interview sheets of two Mexican American women who had applied for teaching jobs with the district. These forms contained statements such as, "spoke without a trace of an accent and looked like an Anglo," or "alright to teach Anglo children." [41]

In July, 1978, the García case ended. Based in part on evidence such as indicated in the tables, Judge Owen D. Cox ruled for the plaintiffs. In a twenty-nine-page statement, the court observed that the VISD should have approximately 50 percent more Mexican American educators than were presently employed and that the district had "purposefully discriminated against Mexican American job applicants." [42] Cox went on to assert that:

> The exclusion of Mexican Americans from the top positions in the Victoria School District, the concentration of Mexican Americans in the lower paying positions in the District, the perception of a lack of upward mobility of Mexican Americans caused by their exclusion from top positions in the District, the failure and refusal to actively recruit and hire Mexican Americans for upper level positions, the lack of a system of informing applicants of openings in higher positions and other practices and policies described in these findings . . . when considered together, lead to the inescapable conclusion of a "prima facie" case of promotion of discrimination in this case. [43]

Cristobal García would have been allowed to seek not only back pay with interest from the district but also employment as a counselor pending the end of the 1978–79 school year (during which he was under contract as a special education counselor for the Goliad School District). Unfortunately, García suffered a fatal heart attack in a Corpus Christi store four months after Cox's ruling. Through the local LULAC branch, the local Mexican American community honored García's memory by instituting a scholarship fund in his name.

García's suit against the VISD was not the last. Another would follow in the 1980s.[44] Due to its intransigent attitude, the VISD would be dragged through the courts again and again, this time at the hands of one of its own members.

Teresa Gutiérrez, a local housewife, was elected in 1985 to represent a single-member district on the south side of town. Prior to 1985 board members were elected at-large citywide. Although each incumbent had a numbered seat on the board, these numbers did not reflect a geographically distinct area within the city in which they lived nor the one they were elected to represent. The theory behind all at-large school board positions was the conventional one: since the electorate picked school board members each would pursue the best general interests of the district rather than an isolated part. The reality was quite different. The at-large system meant that middle-class and wealthy Anglos, who traditionally voted in larger numbers than minorities, could control the school board elections. To be sure, John Artero and Martín Cano had scored victories before 1985. But Artero managed to win because of the large number of white candidates running against him. The uniqueness of the race split the white vote, allowing him, in a sense, to sneak in the back door. Whereas Artero only served one three-year term on the board, Cano served for over a decade, not because he rallied to the cause of Mexican Americans but because once elected he proved himself to be acceptable to white voters and elites. Without their support in an at-large system, it would have been virtually impossible for a minority candidate to have experienced continued success over such a long stretch of time.

In response to pressure by the Mexican American Legal Defense and Educational Fund (MALDEF, founded in 1968) and a small cadre of local activists, the U.S. Justice Department forced the VISD Board to change its electoral structure in 1985. The board's composition went from seven at-large positions to five single-member district posts with the remaining two being at-large. Since there had traditionally been seven board members, each with a numbered seat, the board decided that the new single-member district seats would keep the number of the district (one through five) and each of the two at-large positions would keep the numbers six and seven. But in November of 1986 a three-judge panel found that the two numbered at-large positions "constituted a change affecting voting within the meaning of Section 5 of the Voting Rights Act, requiring pre-clearance from the United States Department of Justice." The judges ordered a special election for the two at-large positions, this time without numbers.[45]

The change in electoral structure opened the door to more equal representation on the board for minority interests. Whereas before only minority candidates who were acceptable to white voters (i.e., disinterested in vocally opposing the status quo), or who managed to run against a large slate of Anglo candidates who split the white vote — as was the case with Artero — had held any hope of winning a school board election, now minority candidates had a fair chance of winning. As a result of outside pressure and intervention, the voters of district five in 1985 elected Teresa Gutiérrez, the first Mexican American woman to serve on the school board.

During her involvement with the PTA Gutiérrez became interested in board politics. As an active PTA member she learned how to abide by parliamentary procedure, address groups, and how to deal with problems affecting African and Mexican American VISD students. She realized early on during her term that Anglo school board members were not concerned about minority issues such as performance gaps between Anglo and minority students or inferior physical plants.

Gutiérrez represented an overwhelmingly minority district and thus acted as the sole voice for minority matters on the school board. Her uncompromisingly principled stance on behalf of the Mexican American and African American electorate frequently clashed with the goals of Anglo board members and their constituents. Further complicating the relationship between Gutiérrez, her supporters, the board, and the larger community was the fact that she behaved in nontraditional ways. Bold, assertive, and confrontational, Gutiérrez's behavior offended some as she rejected the normative role of woman as quiet nurturer. Her strident defense of student and parent interests in her district stirred the pot of racial tension and continually raised sensitive questions that created harsh feelings between her and the Anglo board members. Her outspoken manner, and her dedication to barrio concerns, in addition to a multitude of other factors, emboldened the Mexican American community in Victoria and litigation seemed inevitable. It occurred in 1987.

In the early spring of 1987 Gutiérrez and MALDEF sued the school district over what they perceived to be an unfair change in language on the proposed ballots for the upcoming school board elections. In light of the move to create five single-member seats and two at-large posts, the VISD revised absentee ballots (which originally read "vote for two") to meet the deadline for the beginning of absentee voting on Monday, March 16, 1987. But the wording "vote for two" was misleading as it indicated that voters had to choose two of the candidates listed on the ballot when in fact they could vote for none, one, or two of them. Already the district had been under court order to submit any changes in election procedures (including ballot language) to a federal panel for preclearance. The Justice Department, in reviewing the issue in March, considered enjoining the election until ballot changes were made. In response, district officials conducted a series of telephone interviews and ultimately decided to reword the ballots so that the instructions directed: "vote for not more than two." A local activist named Alex Rojas, however, hardly considered a series of telephone calls as preclearance. Further, Rojas and MALDEF representatives believed that the newly proposed language was still potentially confusing to voters. He hoped to have the ballots changed to read "vote for one or two."[46] In late March, 1987, MALDEF asked for the words "vote for none, one, or two" on the ballot and the three-judge federal panel hearing the ballot language case finally settled on the wording "vote for two or less" in time for the April 4 elections.[47]

Teresa Gutiérrez and many members of the Mexican American community saw in the new controversy yet another attempt by the school board to limit the influence of Mexican Americans daring to exert their rights to equal access to public education. The issue raised the ire of Victorians, both Mexican Americans and Anglos, and it quickly took on racial overtones. Two Mexican Americans invoked their rights as citizens and their roles as taxpayers and patriots, for instance. Arnold Davis, a local businessman and member of the Mexican American Chamber of Commerce, wrote to the *Victoria Advocate* on March 31, 1987, and spoke not of minority rights or racism but of his concern as a taxpayer. Although he never mentioned Gutiérrez by name, he implied support for her position by asking when the school board planned to stop gambling with tax dollars by allowing itself to be dragged through the courts for noncompliance with desegregation and antidiscriminatory policies. He felt that district residents would rather see the money spent on "books, teachers, and equipment and not for unnecessary legal fees."[48] On April 2, 1987, Chris Rivera also addressed the *Victoria*

Chris Rivera, local businessman. *Courtesy Victoria Regional History Center, Victoria College/UH-Victoria Library*

Advocate. Employing republican discourse to criticize Anglo school board members, Rivera argued that the United States was supposed to be a country of laws not of men, but that the majority of school board members had usurped that ideal. Additionally, he pointed out the irony of litigation involving unfair practices toward Mexican Americans during the 200th anniversary of the United States Constitution.

Advancing another opinion, Aquilla Adams also in a letter to the *Advocate* criticized the MALDEF suit over election ballot wording. Invoking images of self-serving banditry, Adams believed that MALDEF was prompting Teresa Gutiérrez to continually sue the district so that MALDEF could line its pockets with school district money. Adams also feared that success by MALDEF only encouraged other Mexican Americans to litigate over the "least little thing."[49] Davis, Rivera, and Adams represented the diversity of opinions over the actions of

MADLEF and Gutiérrez and reflected the increasing polarization caused by Mexican American struggles for change.

Meanwhile, relations between Gutiérrez and the school board deteriorated. In 1986 the widening rift between the two resulted in a new board policy allowing the board president discretionary powers over what could be placed on the board's agenda. The new policy stated that an item could not be placed before the board without either approval from two board members or the permission of the board president himself.[50]

On April 28, 1987, however, five Mexican American voters in VISD asked the district court to convene a three-judge panel to see if VISD's agenda access policy was discriminatory. Represented by MALDEF the voters argued that the agenda procedure created "a new pyramid of authority" on the board. MALDEF declared that the new discretion, by allowing the president wider powers to set the board business, allotted increased strength and representation to 20 percent of the district's electorate, thus correspondingly increasing the clout of the voters from that district. The president was one of seven board members and so only represented 14 percent of the electorate. Once elections were held, furthermore, board members themselves chose one of their own as president. Thus the head of the board, if allowed such authority, theoretically had the ability to override the desires of fellow members who may have wished to address certain issues. Hence, MALDEF lawyers argued the remaining 86 percent of district voters had their power "immeasurably reduced" with the implementation of the new policy. MALDEF further argued that the initiative was intended to silence the voice of the only Hispanic trustee — Teresa Gutiérrez.[51]

On July 7, 1987, superintendent Larry Vaugn and board president Johnny Wilson argued in sworn depositions that the impetus for the policy derived not from a desire to neutralize Gutiérrez but from the efforts to deal with former board member Stephen Bennett, who had resigned his post the previous fall after continually bringing up questions about sex education. Vaugn stated that the sex education issue had been "beaten to death," and the policy was intended to prevent wasting further board time on topics that needed to be put to rest. Asked if there had been high levels of animosity between board members during his tenure as president, Wilson acknowledged in his deposition that there had indeed been difficulties between various members over the sex education matter as well as the suggested closing of William Offer (another south side school) and other schools, but he went on to say that the policy was enacted not to avoid controversy but to deal with unusual problems such as the sex education flap.[52] Yet Joseph E. Reyna, who had lobbied to fill the vacancy on the school board created by Stephen Bennett's resignation, gave contrary testimony in his own deposition, declaring that in meeting with Wilson, the school board president "said he was concerned that certain people kept coming before the Board with the same complaints over and over again." Specifically, Wilson talked about Dwight Harris, "the Black teacher who is Vice-President of the local American Federation of Teachers, Alex Rojas and Wenceslao Gutiérrez [Teresa Gutiérrez's husband]." According to Reyna's statement, Wilson never once mentioned Bennett or the sex education dispute.[53] His testimony and the antagonistic relationship between Gutiérrez and the VISD made the board's argument appear rather specious.

MALDEF and Teresa Gutiérrez emerged victorious on the suit over ballot language in April of 1987, but lost the agenda protest in May, 1988. Although both actions were important on their own merits, they are also significant because of the public reaction they provoked on both sides. Everyday citizens, who might normally have had minimal interest in the activities of the school board, eagerly took sides on the controversies. Mexican Americans were upset over what they perceived as unending attempts by the school board to limit their access to and influence on public institutions. Many Anglo-Americans complained about what they perceived as unending bellyaching by a group of people who sought not equality but preferential treatment. It seems fitting that some of the most intense struggles over these opposing perspectives should have centered on the public schools. After all it was the schools that were responsible for fostering good citizenship and instilling American values.[54]

THE RELATIONSHIP between the VISD and the Mexican American community throughout the twentieth century was tense at best, deeply antagonistic at worst. The fact that race was the primary influence on people's perceptions and actions in Victoria (as well as in much of the state) was mirrored in the schools. Although overt segregation was outlawed in 1954, and equal access to district facilities was mandated through the Civil Rights Act of 1964, the VISD continued to resist compliance with these directives. Despite continued pressure from the public and later from school board trustee Teresa Gutiérrez, the percentage of minority teachers in the district had risen only minimally by the early 1990s when VISD teachers were 77 percent white, 6 percent African American, and 16 percent Hispanic.[55] The hostile nature of the relationship between Anglo teachers and administrators on the one hand, and Mexican American students on the other, has not disappeared. The same type of discouraging circumstances and insurmountable obstacles to success that Mexican American students faced earlier in the century persist to the present.[56]

Couching their arguments in various rhetorical strategies designed to obfuscate an underlying racism, the school board became the instrument through which local whites attempted to enforce a two-tiered educational system. Ironically, the school district that operated according to a limited version of citizenship and sought to teach minority students their "proper" place in society found that many Mexican Americans had absorbed far more than it had intended. Various segments of the Mexican American community came to develop their own definition of citizenship and how to successfully challenge efforts by the school system to hinder that vision. The first steps in that direction were taken by Manuel Velasco and John Artero whose mere presence on the school board represented important victories. But their public profiles and the tensions between whites and Mexican Americans prevented them from engaging in a broad attack on discriminatory policies within the district.

Over time other Mexican Americans learned that the only way to bring about change was to take advantage of the political and judicial tools available to them as Americans, thus expanding previously extant notions of what it meant to be an American. They appealed to nationwide organizations such as LULAC and MALDEF to work in conjunction with active working-class Mexican Americans such as Teresa Gutiérrez to challenge persistent inequalities in the 1980s. At times the stakes were too high. Gutiérrez, for instance, found herself frequently outnumbered in school board decisions. She also faced a measure of backlash within the Mexican American community. Many believed that although she was often right in her accusations she was also often wrong and thus created a hostile climate within the district's policy-making bodies that forestalled educational gains for Mexican Americans.

4

"By the Power of Reason"

The Role of Community-Based Mexican American

Organizations on Identity Formation, 1940–85

THROUGHOUT the post–World War II period, Mexican Americans formed clubs and associations designed to help them carve out a place of equality in Victoria.[1] Some such organizations were working class in composition; in others, the middle class dominated. Despite material or ideological differences among Mexican Americans, those organizations in Victoria functioned in similar manners and shared goals and outlooks. Notwithstanding that these affiliates developed slightly variegated American identities, they all reflected desires to redefine unspoken definitions of normative and prove Mexican American faithfulness to American traditions. Yet, militance typical of the Mexican American experience in other locations appears anomalous in Victoria. Why, then, did accommodation reign in the city? Why did the kinds of militant actions manifested elsewhere not spread to Victoria?

This chapter will examine five different groups active in the city from 1947 through 1985 and will demonstrate that "resistance" in Victoria was shaped by a consensual understanding of citizenship, a view fostered by the dominant society and which the Mexican American community embraced. The first, and perhaps most significant of these organizations was the American Citizens' Social Club (ACSC), which lasted for about thirty years after 1947 before factionalism produced its demise. A second organization to attract a following in Victoria was the local branch of the American G.I. Forum; it advanced a moderate/accommodative vision of resistance to the marginalization of Mexican Americans. Also active in Victoria for a time was the Amalgamated Clothing Workers of America (ACWA); it offered the promise of protecting worker dignity and gave the Victoria community an alternative voice for resisting racism and class oppression. LULAC had a brief and relatively subdued presence in Victoria in the 1950s. But local civic-minded individuals created visible, more active branches in the 1970s and 1980s. Still another association to take up the struggle for equal rights in the city was the de León club. Launched in 1967 primarily to raise money for scholarships to assist local Mexican American college students, the club also attempted to forge a bond with the dominant white middle-class community. Almost none of these organizations proposed radical alternatives for improving the lot of local Mexican Americans.

Years of marginalization combined with the struggle against fascist tyranny in World War II and the newly developing cold war helped to foster a sense of Mexican Americanism in Victoria: an identity that was steeped in patriotism and popular concepts of normative behaviors. Thus aroused, Hispanic Victorians attempted to broaden definitions of citizenship and developed widely acceptable notions of Mexican Americanism, but always as patriots. Apart from limited Chicano activism in the 1960s and 1970s, and a very brief Saul Alinsky–type Catholic organization in the 1980s (detailed earlier in chapter 2), the only example of coordinated overt resistance to the status quo was the aforementioned short-lived clothing workers' union.

THE FIRST formal Mexican American political and civil rights organization in Victoria was the American Citizens' Social Club (ACSC). Formed in 1947 during a meeting at the local Mexican American Catholic Church (Our Lady of Sorrows) the ACSC from the beginning sought improved conditions for Mexican Americans. From the very beginning the club stood as a predominantly working-class organization, a trait it maintained throughout its existence.[2] The original constitution provided for annual dues of about $1 per year. This dues limit was consciously designed to open the club to a wide segment of the Mexican American community.[3] Over the next thirty years, the ACSC and its offshoot would indeed help secure a larger place in American society for Mexican Americans while at the same time negotiating existing concepts of Americanism.

The founders of the American Citizens' Social Club emphasized both their traditional culture and their identity as American citizens. Their constitution read in Spanish and the membership conducted their meetings in a mixture of both languages. Additionally, founding members intentionally chose the name "American Citizens' Social Club" to emphasize their sense of American nationalism and allegiance. In so doing they combined a pride in their ethnicity with a strong sense of patriotism. They planned to serve the interests of the Mexican American community not as a special group asking for favorable attention but rather as a people who had been historically downtrodden and who now sought to gain access to the rights and responsibilities of American citizenship.[4] This desire for equal status in Victoria was part of a larger movement around Texas and the Southwestern United States then being driven by the Mexican American G.I. generation. This cohort of leaders included individuals who had come of age politically during the post–World War II era. They and their family members had developed an enhanced sense of themselves as loyal Americans deserving of constitutional protections. Hence the emergence of the ACSC at this time was reflective of parallel sentiments around the state and nation in the immediate postwar years.

The ACSC is historically significant because its deeds and endeavors point to the ways in which the Mexican American struggle for public legitimacy in Victoria represented the diversity of activism manifest in other parts of the country. ACSC members clearly felt aggrieved with Victoria society yet their anger was focused not on mainstream structures or institutions but rather on particular individuals and discrete portions of society such as businesses. Like the various Mexican American leaders and organizations mentioned in chapters 2, 3, and 5, the ACSC accepted the American political process and free enterprise system. It sought to gain increased access to the benefits of a society based on the principle that education served as the vehicle for upward mobility. It postulated that education would allow their children to compete more equally with their Anglo-American counterparts. That capitalism or democracy, or the republic itself should ever be challenged,

Ralph Rojas, Sr., and Ralph Rojas, Jr. The senior Rojas served during WWII, his son in Vietnam. *Courtesy Beatrice C. Rojas*

was never uttered. From ACSC members' perspective, it was local personalities or institutions that had betrayed the concepts of egalitarianism that formed the basis of Anglo-American society.[5]

Among the ACSC's unique features was its dedication to benevolence. Few other organizations in the city promoted such an interest. There was a Woodsmen of the World (los Hacheros) present in the Victoria area, but it appears to have never gone beyond the narrow function of providing insurance benefits. The ACSC, however, included in its constitution a provision that all members would, in addition to annual dues, be required to donate $1 annually to a mutual benefit fund to be given to the family if a member should die.[6] In 1960 the club expanded the concept of mutuality and formed a special committee that developed a mutual aid plan to provide assistance for hospitalized members.[7]

Beatrice Rojas, wife of Ralph Rojas, Sr., also served in the military in WWII. These photos are representative of a military past that defined the Mexican American historical experience. Mexican American families often placed photos of family members in uniform in prominent places in the living areas of their homes. Not only did such photos express pride in military service, they also manifested a growing patriotism. *Courtesy Beatrice C. Rojas*

Over the years the ACSC grew increasingly appealing to Mexican Americans, both in Victoria and the immediate area. By 1964 the ACSC drew members from the surrounding communities of Tivoli, Port Lavaca, and Placedo. By 1965 the club had mushroomed in size, claiming over 700 members.[8] Its appeal derived from the benefits it offered to its membership and from its political action. In 1960, in stark contrast to the nonpartisan stance of other organizations (such as LULAC nationally, and the de León club locally), the ACSC joined the "Viva Kennedy" movement and endorsed the Democratic presidential ticket.[9] This endorsement of the Kennedy slate, however, was the only example of official endorsement of a candidate and did not mean that the club regularly got involved in political partisanship. Actually, one of its most important political functions was disseminating information to club members and local voters by sponsoring campaign rallies before elections. Candidates for office (local, state, and national) were invited to club meetings to present their platforms. And while individual club members might have endorsed specific candidates in public, the ACSC never took sides in these races and never used its power to organize a large block of voters in order to persuade candidates into taking any particular stand on specific issues.[10]

Another significant activity that drew the ACSC's attention were poll tax drives designed to increase Mexican American political involvement. ACSC members went door to door and canvassed residents for payments of the tax, then a requirement for voting. In 1962, for example, the ACSC planned to arm "4,000 of our citizens with a poll tax."[11] As an incentive to these purchases, the club also held dances for which the only cover charge was a poll tax receipt.[12] In order to better utilize the club's growing influence in the Mexican American community the ACSC began developing connections with and inviting important political figures to speak at its functions. Thus in 1968 and 1969, for example, United States representative Henry B. González and United States senator Ralph Yarbrough addressed the group's annual anniversary banquets.[13]

Numerous other features distinguished the ACSC from existing clubs in the city. For instance, the ACSC was family oriented, and thus did not see a reason to develop a separate auxiliary organization for women or children. This is not to argue that the ACSC was leading the fight for gender equity. Full membership did not immediately translate into equal status. Thus the organization's early leadership was composed of men. Women were counted as full members and were allowed to vote on club issues and speak freely at meetings but not to take leadership responsibilities. Activities within the club, therefore, fell along traditional gender divisions. One example of this can be found in the fundraising bingos. Men organized and supervised the events while women cooked and worked in the kitchen.[14] By the 1970s, however, women took a larger role in the organization, attaining official leadership positions within the group. Such gains did not threaten established gender boundaries as early women officers served as club secretary or club treasurer. But these steps opened the door to further advancement so that by the 1970s the club had its first woman president.[15]

Perhaps the American Citizens' Social Club's most enduring legacy was its belief in promoting education for Mexican American students. The ACSC's constitution included provisions for the creation of a Public Education Committee that was to monitor relationships between the Mexican American community and the public school system. Additionally, the club raised funds to pay for such school-related items as supplies, band equipment, and field trips. These efforts were instrumental in urging Mexican American children take part in traditional school activities and in helping them to fit into the academic mainstream.[16]

Beyond these efforts, the ACSC helped expand the growing Mexican American middle class through its scholarship program. Initially, holding dances and presenting pageants raised scholarship money. But in the 1960s club members decided to try bingo, a move that turned out to be a very lucrative proposition for the club. Because of bingo, the club was able to increase dramatically its scholarship funding as well as to put away money that was eventually used to purchase land and erect a building for club meetings and functions.[17] Unfortunately, as the club began to see increasing levels of economic success it also began to experience internal dissension. In part the rift developed over the funds raised through bingo and the use of revenue derived therefrom.

One faction within the club, the old guard led by Carlos Solís, became concerned with what it considered lax, inefficient bookkeeping methods by a newer generation of leadership as represented by Matt López. An inability to account adequately for all bingo receipts created an air of distrust between the old guard and the emerging rival faction. Indeed, it would later be discovered that some club money had been diverted to help at least one member of the emerging opposition pay personal debts.[18] Such alleged malfeasance led the old guard to fear that the credibility of the ACSC was being undermined.

Further fueling tensions was the fact that some members believed that less money was being funneled through the bingo games to the scholarship fund. This concern made many older members fear that the pro-bingo wing in the club was losing sight of the organization's original goals. These traditionalists further worried that such behavior threatened to turn the ACSC into a self-serving group interested in socializing and raising money simply to fill the ACSC coffers, or worse yet, to enrich the bingo supporting faction. The rival faction within the club, comprised of somewhat younger, newer members, argued that nothing unethical was afoot. Moreover, they believed that the club was in danger of becoming stagnant if it did not continue to grow, and one important method to ensure continued growth, so the argument ran, was through the more efficient management of the bingo operations.

But bingo games and bingo money were not the only sticking points between the two groups: personalities soon came into play. During the ACSC meeting of December, 1969, in light of a disagreement between the old guard and the rival faction over financial reports and election procedures, Solís predicted the club's downfall. By this time personal relations between the two competing camps had deteriorated to such a point that an alternative group of officers (comprised of the old guard) had begun acting in place of the officers elected the previous year. Additionally, tensions had mounted such that the Sheriff's office had been asked to guard the ACSC bingos, even though it did not do so for the other bingo clubs in town.[19]

Another area of dispute between the two rival parties involved elections. In December, 1968, the organization supposedly elected a new slate of officers comprised of the bingo supporters: Matt López as president, Ralph Castillo as vice-president, and Pete Cantú as treasurer. The old faction questioned whether the ACSC had held legal elections and argued that the new leadership was illegitimate. When pressed for documentation of such elections, the upstarts initially claimed that voting was carried out by acclamation and that records had been lost. Later, however, they turned over minutes that included discussions for the December meetings of 1969 and 1970 (elections were held each December) that showed that López, Castillo, and Cantú had been elected by the membership in each of those years. The old guard, however, charged that by poorly publicizing the elections the opposition hid them from the general membership. Thus in 1970 the nominating committee agreed to renominate only the present officers (López, Castillo, and Cantú) for reelection.[20] But the infighting that had plagued the club since 1968 took its toll on the club's membership. The ACSC had boasted 700 members a few years earlier, but by 1970 listed only forty-two members, with an active core of about six.[21]

In September of 1971 the old guard held an unauthorized election and announced a new slate of officers for an organization called the American Citizens' Social Club Incorporated (ACSCI) that claimed itself as legal heir to the assets of the American Citizens' Social Club. The new organization argued that the ACSC as presently operating had digressed from the club's original community service orientation and that the ACSCI now sought to bring the old ACSC back to its first principles.[22] But the ACSC countered in January, 1972, with a restraining order limiting its rival's usage of the ACSC's property.[23] Eventually it became clear that the two groups were so far apart that only a lawsuit would be able to settle the dispute.[24]

Finally, on July 25, 1973, an out-of-court settlement stipulated that the old guard (ACSCI) would be allowed to receive $1,200 in contested club assets and to maintain the name American Citizens' Social Club Incorporated. The settlement permitted the other group (ACSC under the leadership of the rival faction) to control the remainder of the club's assets but it had to change its name.[25] Eventually, it became the United Citizens' Club. As late as spring 1979 the American Citizens' Social Club donated $4,100 in scholarships to twenty-nine college students, twenty-two of whom attended Victoria College.[26] But the factionalism and the infighting that led to the split had debilitated the leadership of both organizations so that by 1980 neither would ever serve as an effective voice of leadership in the Mexican American community.

The split experienced by the ACSC indicated the differing visions of the role such civic organizations should play in Victoria. The old guard continued its focus on political empowerment, education, and community service. The rival faction emphasized fundraising activities and social events. To be sure, the latter group also wanted to contribute money to Mexican American college students, and believed that the lucrative bingos were the best way to raise funds. Yet it lacked the deeper sense of social vision expressed by its rival. The old guard sought ways to make politicians accountable to the Mexican American community and to increase a sense of civic mindedness among its membership. The challengers, by contrast, turned inward by, for example, becoming less politically active and using funds for items such as a new meeting hall. Well before the collapse of the American Citizens' Social Club, however, Mexican Americans in Victoria had turned to another larger organization that expressed a similarly gradualist approach to social change, but motivated by a deeply rooted sense of patriotism and antiradicalism.

THE AMERICAN G.I. Forum established a chapter in Victoria in 1954, six years after its founding by Dr. Hector P. García in Corpus

Christi, Texas.[27] Sharing the same worldview as Dr. García, local World War II veterans immediately set about creating a college scholarship fund that they financed by a pancake supper and benefit barbecue. One year later they bestowed the first of many such scholarships to Alfred Borrego. The scholarship provided for two years of funding at the Victoria Junior College and two years of upper division coursework at the institution of Borrego's choosing.[28] The following year, the Forum was able to provide scholarships for five additional students.[29]

Such a commitment to educating youths reflected the value that the organizationally minded, vocal segments of the Mexican American community placed on schooling as a means of attaining upward mobility. Members of the AGIF in Victoria believed that increasing Mexican Americans' access to higher education would help develop a coterie of Mexican American middle-class professionals who could make significant contributions to the larger community, thereby garnering a more respectable and equitable space in society for all Mexican Americans. This goal of increasing the Mexican American presence in the local middle class was one shared by most other Mexican American organizations in the city. And just as the AGIF reflected common goals embraced by the more articulate segments of the Mexican American community, it also displayed an adherence to widely accepted attitudes toward gender roles.

Unlike the ACSC, the state AGIF developed a separate auxiliary for women and another for young adults by 1949. The purpose of these auxiliary units was to provide a way for veterans' family members to participate in the struggle for equality as well as to mobilize people for work other than the raising of scholarship funds. Assisted by these reserve units the Victoria chapter of the AGIF took on projects besides helping future aspirants become part of the middle class. They and their auxiliaries solicited donations from local businesses, sponsored events such as a "turkey shoot," and held benefit dances, talent shows, and special motion picture showings, all for the purpose of assisting local needy children with such items as clothing and school supplies.

While the Forum may have been touted as a radical organization by those who sought to maintain a segregated, unequal society, the fact of the matter was that from the very beginning, the Forum was dedicated to supporting the dominant values of American society, its political system, and its economic structures. Dr. García made explicit the principle that his organization sought to work within the existing parameters of American society to bring about evolutionary change. By engaging in activities such as "pay your poll tax campaigns" and "back to school drives," the AGIF promoted civic mindedness and a sense of ownership in American society. In the process the AGIF shunned the idea of militance and downplayed its role as a defender of an oppressed group. Indeed, García himself acknowledged distaste for the phrase "civil rights" and for the growing tendency through the 1950s by people to consider the AGIF as primarily a civil rights organization.[30]

Hence the Victoria AGIF's goal was never to challenge the basic foundations of American society. In fact it went out of its way to support the ideal. When the International Union of Mine, Mill and Smelter Workers sent a copy of its news organ, *The Union*, to Forum headquarters in Corpus Christi in early 1954, executive secretary Ed Idar wrote to *The Union's* editor requesting that Mine Mill refrain from any future communication with the Forum. In presenting his case, Idar stated that,

> This organization takes pride in its record of service to the Mexican American Veteran and his family but at the same time it takes pride in being made up of members who are loyal to their country and who have fought for it. We have no [*sic*] sympathy for an organization whose loyalty is primarily to a foreign power and to a foreign ideology that stands directly opposed to every principle of Democracy.[31]

Five years later García sent a memo to all chapters of the AGIF including a list, provided by the House Un-American Activities Committee, of allegedly subversive organizations operating in the United States. The memo asks members to "be thorough in your screening process to keep communists and subversives from our ranks. Notice the kind remarks sent to us by J. Edgar Hoover. I believe that you should feel as proud as I do for receiving this letter."[32]

In Victoria the AGIF expressed its views on loyalty and citizenship by trying to bring the foreign born into the fold. In 1957 and 1958, for instance, the Victoria AGIF sponsored citizenship instruction for individuals seeking naturalization. Their first class included not only several Mexican immigrants but also a war bride from Germany and another from Japan.[33] For Victoria Forumeers, citizenship meant indoctrinating people with patriotism, helping the less privileged, and naturalizing new citizens. It did not entail confronting and questioning the democratic, capitalist system directly.[34] But while civic-oriented organizations were leveling subtle challenges to a discriminatory status quo, embracing fundamental mainstream values, and distancing themselves from any overt forms of ideological or methodological radicalism another group was forming in the early 1970s that struck out at one of the most fundamental aspects of free market capitalism — the relationship between workers and owners.

In May of 1970, the Farah company (a clothing manufacturer that made slacks and operated plants in San Antonio, El Paso, and New Mexico) announced with great fanfare that it was opening a plant in Victoria and would ultimately employ over 1,000 workers.[35] When it started business in the fall of 1971, the Farah factory was widely hailed as a new source of employment and as a generator of business taxes for the area. The Chamber of Commerce and other business leaders could not have anticipated the emergence of a labor movement following such a seemingly serendipitous addition to the city.

Most of the workers at the Farah plant in Victoria were women. They did the actual sewing of the pants, but men did the cutting from the patterns, moved the material and finished products around, and loaded and unloaded trucks. There were few if any African Americans at the compound: the workforce was predominantly Mexican American with some Anglo-Americans.[36] While the integrated labor force worked amicably, future events drove a wedge between Anglo and Mexican American workers.

Even as the Chamber of Commerce had held its celebratory reception to announce the opening of the plant, the Amalgamated Clothing Workers of America (ACWA) had been trying to organize in several Farah branches in Texas and New Mexico in 1969. In May, 1972, the ACWA began unionizing efforts at Farah in Victoria. The chief in-plant union organizer there was Daniel Delgado, a bundle-boy and inspector.[37] His efforts were none too easy, however. There was a fear among some of the Mexican American workers that joining the union would cost them their jobs. Anglo employees harbored similar anxiety;

moreover, they resented that the union drive was being headed and abetted by Mexican American workers.[38]

Almost immediately the company supposedly began harassing those suspected of union activity. On some occasions its staff threatened to release activists involved in unionizing efforts. At other times managers photographed those in the act of passing out union literature. This last tactic severely hampered the recruitment drives. Without photographers around workers accepted the union leaflets being distributed, but with photographers around they shied away from what might be inferred as collusion with the activists. Not all were intimidated, however.[39] Many joined the ACWA by picketing three clothing stores in Victoria that sold Farah products: Beall's department store; Melvin's Globe Clothiers; and Dunlap's.[40]

Tensions came to a peak in January, 1973, when the national ACWA filed a complaint through the National Labor Relations Board (NLRB) against the Victoria Farah plant for unfair labor practices. In the action the ACWA charged that Farah had engaged in unfair and illegal practices such as interrogating workers about union activity; banning pro-union solicitation during nonworking hours; threatening to discharge workers for union support; creating a hostile, anti-union environment by distributing pro-company buttons (called happy badges); photographing picket line activity; and firing twenty-four workers on the union organizing committee.[41]

Ultimately, the federal court hearing the NLRB complaint, on January 30, 1973, found Farah guilty of the above charges and ordered the company to stop its anti-union practices. Further, the court directed Farah to print and post a notice to its employees stating that it would cease and desist actions aimed at intimidating union supporters.[42]

Then on November 1, 1973, workers at the Farah plant received a bolt from the blue. Farah announced that it was closing its plants in Victoria and El Paso, Texas, as well as in Las Cruces, New Mexico. The Victoria site received notice thirty minutes after lunch on Thursday, November 1, that the plant would shut down immediately.[43] According to Farah the closings were a response to declining sales brought about by the boycott instigated in July, 1972, by "the Amalgamated Clothing Workers' Union, the AFL-CIO and its Church supporters." The release claimed that the clothing giant was only reacting to market conditions brought on by the boycott, not retaliating for the boycott and organizational activities of the union. Yet in the body of the press release, Farah stated that

> union officials have gloated and taken credit for downturns in our profit picture. I wonder if they are now prepared to rejoice publicly that their campaign of falsehood, vilification, and the systematic harassment of retailers throughout the country has succeeded in putting 600 people out of work [in two states] — most of them women and a large majority American citizens of Mexican ancestry.

Farah further declared that it was engaging in a struggle for popular public opinion, or as it called it, a "battle of communications." Simultaneously, it tried to lay claim to the moral high ground by blaming the entire incident and its repercussions on the union and its supporters.[44]

This was the only (and last) episode involving a predominantly Mexican American labor movement in Victoria. For the people involved in the Farah plant incident, labor activism grew to be an important part of their lives, at least briefly. The Farah workers had used the ACWA to express their own version of "working-class Americanism," one that subordinated the status of the individual and capital to the need for collective economic justice.[45] But many other Mexican Americans looked negatively upon the Farah unionists. The majority remained influenced by a traditional southern anti-labor bias. They denied widespread community support to the activists because unionism, in their minds, went against the grain of mainstream free market values that constituted a substantial aspect of the ideological foundation of citizenship. The local media, furthermore, focused on the rights of private property and the loss of jobs that resulted from Farah's desire to avoid unionized workers at all costs.[46]

SHORTLY AFTER the failed organizational efforts at Farah, and at a time when the ACSC was in steep decline, Mexican Americans found another recourse in their efforts toward developing and promoting views of citizenship. Victoria's first highly visible and active LULAC chapter, Council 626, was formed in the mid-1970s, composed primarily of middle-class and upper-working-class members who shared the organization's vision for the creation of an integrated, racially cooperative society. Council 626 members sought to take part in mainstream life and focused on problems outside the immediate concern of the Mexican American community. This broader scope stemmed from Mexican American desires to reach out to the larger community and to become more active participants in advancing American bountifulness. Just as the national organization frequently sought to address mainstream issues as a way of claiming a more central place in American society, so too did Council 626 seek to carve out a public space for itself as defender of all citizens, not just the Spanish speaking.

For example, in September of 1977 the Council sent a letter to the administrator of Care Inn South, a local nursing home, charging the institution with thirteen serious deficiencies. Among the problems listed were inadequate staffing, unsanitary conditions, irregular visits by doctors, and frequent falls by patients. The Council also included a list of nine suggestions for improvement.[47] Such LULAC interests did not simply involve Mexican American patients, nor did they arise out of ethnic issues. Council president Alex López emphasized that none of the charges were "racial in nature." According to council members, 90 percent of the citizens who came to LULAC with information regarding inadequacies at the nursing home were white. Additionally, District X director Roque "Rocky" Martínez argued that the Council thought "our senior citizens—Anglo, Mexican-American or whatever they may be—deserve more than [inadequate care]."[48]

Indeed, LULAC was not the only player involved in leveling charges at the nursing home. Former Victoria County judge Joe Bumgardner revealed that he too had lodged a complaint regarding similar problems with the Texas Department of Human Resources (TDHR) in February on behalf of a local couple whom he did not identify by name.[49] Another charge was filed by a Mrs. Jean Dabney whose mother had been a patient at the home. Dabney's grievance led to an investigation by the Houston branch of the TDHR, while the LULAC allegation resulted in a probe by the Corpus Christi branch of the TDHR. Ultimately, the investigations found it difficult to substantiate all of the accusations, although it identified seven deficiencies.[50]

Despite LULAC Council 626's strides in taking an active part in community issues, the LULAC movement was soon stalled by internecine conflict. In 1977 a rift formed among various members of Council 626. The split resulted from a philosophical disagreement, exacerbated by personal animosities. One segment of Council 626 wanted to maintain its focus on community-based needs, while a competing group within the Council preferred to concentrate more closely on issues immediately affecting Mexican Americans, similar to ones undertaken by the ACSC. These philosophical issues quickly became personalized as evident in correspondence sent to Rubén Bonilla, then national president of LULAC. The rival faction within Council 626 subsequently argued successfully for the creation of a new LULAC chapter in Victoria.[51] Hence in 1978 the presence of the new Council, number 4319, diffused Mexican American activism in the city and diluted the strength of Council 626. Additionally, the untimely death in 1978 of District X director Roque Martínez, who had been a driving force in Council 626, significantly contributed to his council's eventual demise.[52] But then new LULAC 4319 immediately began to execute its plans in behalf of ethnic improvement.

Rather than engaging in cooperative efforts with other minority organizations such as the National Association for the Advancement of Colored People (NAACP), or becoming involved in broader issues such as had Council 626 in investigating the Care Inn South, Council 4319 sought to consolidate its efforts on concerns more immediately touching on the Mexican American community. Thus the two primary goals of Council 4319 were to increase voter registration within the Mexican American community and to raise money for college scholarships.[53]

These activities did not negate LULAC's general desire to work within the existing social order for evolutionary change as well as its desire for middle-class respectability. Council 4319, for example, unofficially organized its members and their friends to walk door to door through predominantly Mexican American neighborhoods on the south side of the city encouraging adults to register and vote. While the LULAC constitution forbade any formal partisan activities in the name of the organization, former Council 4319 member Lupita Hernández recalled that, "We met with friends . . . we didn't do it through LULAC . . . we did it on our own because we weren't allowed to endorse."[54] Thus LULAC's presence acted as a coalescing agent for politically minded Mexican Americans in Victoria and helped them create a network through which they could engage in political movements. In this way LULACers sought to encourage Mexican Americans to take part in the political process without officially embracing a particular party or ideology.

And while encouraging political activism within the Mexican American community was important to the members of Council 4319, they turned most of their attention to raising college scholarship funds for local Mexican American students. They did so by holding benefit dances, but an early tactic for raising such funds was to hold "midnight bingos" at the Club Westerner, a local dance hall. Our Lady of Sorrows, the Mexican Catholic church, held its fundraising bingos on Friday and Saturday nights. So in order to take advantage of the market for bingo addicts and avoid competing with the church, the Council held their events on Friday after the church bingos had ended at 11:00 p.m. Throughout its twelve-year existence Council 4319 raised several thousands of dollars for local Mexican American college students.

The role LULAC expected to play in the future of Victoria's Mexican American community was highlighted by the creation of the Cris García Memorial Scholarship Banquet in 1984. The banquet was held to preserve the memory of the aforementioned Cris García, a former teacher for the Victoria Independent School District who after several failed attempts at promotion won a class action suit that opened the doors of employment for Mexican Americans seeking professional positions within the district as teachers, counselors, and administrators. Although García had died in the summer of 1983 he had remained an important part of popular memory for many Mexican Americans in Victoria after his death.[55] During the awards banquet of 1988 the theme of education that García held dear was reiterated by guest speaker Manuel Pacheco, president of the University of Houston–Downtown. "Education continues to be important to mainstream Americans," Pacheco asserted in reference to the Mexican American community and in focusing attention on the need to address the rising dropout rate among Mexican Americans.[56]

Council 4319 poses an interesting topic of study due to its unique structure. Scholarly studies of LULAC have concluded that LULAC chapters tended toward middle-class composition and perspective. In contrast, Council 4319 consisted of both middle- and working-class members. Moreover, the Council's leadership reflected the cross-class composition of the rank and file. Both classes sought to find ways to bring about changes without threatening the basic structures of society or without even threatening the white power elite. Further, this cross-class coalition attests to the lack of class-consciousness in Victoria that might have allowed for middle-class worldviews and values to overshadow all other perspectives. The lack of alternatives for local Mexican Americans explains the class integration in Council 4319. By the mid-1970s the American Citizens' Social Club was in decline. The local Mexican American Chamber of Commerce had a different function than did LULAC or ACSC. Thus rather than start from scratch, local individuals wanting to become active in helping the Mexican American community looked to LULAC. After all, it was a nationally recognized organization with over fifty years of activism to offer.

The presence of women in leadership positions in Council 4319 also marked it as distinct in terms of other Mexican American organizations in the city and around the nation. Dr. Anita del Río's run for the national presidency of LULAC in 1985, for example, marked only the second time in LULAC's history that a woman ran for that position. It is true that the American G.I. Forum allowed women to participate in their activities, but only through the Ladies Auxiliary. It is also true that the American Citizens' Social Club in Victoria had its first and only woman president in the previous decade. But Council 4319 appeared to have groomed women to be leaders in the community.[57] In fact a majority of its officers were often women.[58]

Despite cross-class solidarity and a practice of gender equity, a dedicated core of members that acted as the driving force behind the Council, and the continued need for local activism by Mexican Americans, LULAC Council 4319 began experiencing a downturn in membership by the late 1980s. For example, the Council boasted twenty-seven members in 1985, but this figure had dropped to only eighteen in 1987.[59] Interest in LULAC in the Golden Crescent region had been fading fast as early as the spring of 1979. Port Lavaca, a town with a population of under 10,000 located twenty-five miles to the south, had a council that could not even hold elections because of diminishing membership. According to Roque Martínez, all the councils in the district were lax in paying dues and "the treasurer's books [were] messed up . . . people will not show up for meetings, will not attend state level functions, etc."[60] The most important factor in this decline in membership and interest had been national developments in LULAC's internal politics.

Political scientist Benjamin Márquez has noted how LULAC, nationally, had been losing supporters and experiencing a growing dependence on governmental and corporate sponsorship through the 1970s. The late 1970s and early 1980s, however, augured a rejuvenation for LULAC under the direction of Texans Rubén Bonilla, his brother Tony, and California's Mario Obledo.[61] Despite the dynamic leadership provided by these three individuals the organization suffered from a continuing lack of grass-roots economic backing (such as that identified by Roque Martínez), which forced LULAC to search for outside sources of revenue. Additionally, the organization took a conservative turn in 1985 with the election of Oscar Morán as national president.

These internal problems by the national LULAC caused members of Victoria LULAC Council 4319 to question their affiliation with an organization that appeared unable to sustain itself both in terms of economic solvency and political consistency. While LULAC at the local and national level proclaimed a dedication to remaining above partisan politics, the reality was that the political ideologies of the two major parties shaped LULAC's national internal politics. LULAC members around the country found the conservative approach taken by some LULAC presidents acceptable, but others found it distasteful and thus members' interest waned. As a result of this kind of institutional turmoil in the national hierarchy, Council 4319 decided not to renew its charter in 1990.[62] But the demise of both Victoria LULAC councils did not mean the end of Mexican American organization in Victoria. By the time Council 4319 had been created, another Mexican American politically oriented organization that proved internally cohesive and stable had been in operation for almost a decade.

THE DE LEÓN CLUB was organized in Victoria in June of 1967. The *Victoria Advocate* described it then as a "new service club composed of business and professional men."[63] Like LULAC, the de León Club from its inception was an organization with a deeply entrenched middle-class perspective. Two closely related aspects of the de León Club's activities point toward this middle-class standard.[64]

First, the de León Club established a college scholarship fund financed primarily through two annual dances, one held during the summer and one during the Christmas season. By 1973 the club reportedly raised a minimum of $1,600 from its Christmas dance alone. As with the scholarship efforts of the ACSC and LULAC Council 4319, the de León Club also hoped to contribute to a growing professional class within Victoria's Mexican American community.

The de León Club dances confirm the organization's middle-class inclinations. Traditionally, the Mexican American middle class, not just in Victoria but also throughout the state, had recognized its difference from the working class. One central aspect of this process of differentiation was the kind of music each group preferred. While traditional conjunto music that centers on the accordion was considered the province of workers, middle-class Mexican Americans developed a preference for orchestral music. This taste for the orchestra was reflected in the bands the club contracted to play for the annual benefit dances. Bands that performed at de León dances included Eddie Galván and His Orchestra, the Noé Pro Orchestra, and the Paul Elizondo Orchestra.[65]

These bands played primarily Mexican and Spanish orchestral tunes, which reflected the fact that members of the de León Club, while conscious of their middle-class status, held deep roots in their Mexican past. Although the de León Club's constitution was written in English, members maintained a pride in their culture and continued to speak Spanish and promote Mexican or Spanish festivities. Also, the club developed a long-running association with the University of Houston, Victoria, and together the two have sponsored the annual de León Symposium since 1987. Each spring, a joint committee invites scholars to present papers on various aspects of the Mexican American experience to the general public. This conference has served as a forum for creating public awareness of the contributions of Mexican Americans to American society and culture.[66]

The de León Club sought middle-class acceptance and respectability by promoting a professional public image of Mexican Americans and by engaging in community service that extended beyond the boundaries of the Mexican American community. In the 1970s the club got involved in philanthropic causes that targeted the needs of such organizations as the Boys' Club, the public library, the local Catholic high school, and the city's parks department.[67] By the early 1980s the club had grown in size and influence so that in 1982, for example, the membership donated over $34,000 to worthy causes apart from its scholarship program.[68]

The activities of the de León Club reflected one aspect of the sense of identity that had formed among Victoria's Mexican American middle class. Similar to companion middle-class organizations around the state and the nation, the de León Club sought to confirm its own image as an all-American organization. And while clinging to its past and its culture the club also embraced a vision of its place in society that involved greater levels of interaction with the Anglo-American establishment. Similar to LULAC, the de León Club sought an integrationist approach to equality and never questioned the nation's basic political or economic foundations. Their way was seeking a gradual reform of social problems primarily through self-help, as with college funding, and through reaching out to the wider community in attempts to gain respectability for the Mexican community.

WHILE MEXICAN AMERICANS across the Southwest had been organizing into *mutualistas*, labor unions, and various civic and political organizations since the turn of the century, Mexican Americans in Victoria did not take such steps on a comparable scale until after World War II. Beginning with the ACSC in 1947, however, Victoria's Mexican American population began a process of organization and activism designed to promote its bicultural views of American citizenship.

The working-class members of the American Citizens' Social Club, as did members of other groups, sought to encourage the growth of a Mexican American professional class through a scholarship program. Although composed mostly of workers, it had middle-class ambitions for American youth. Yet it also focused on the needs of underprivileged Mexican American school-aged children by providing funds for school supplies and extracurricular functions. But the nonpartisan political activism of the club testified to the club's dedication to the two-party system and an acceptance of the American political system in general. Over time, the club came to embrace greater levels of gender equity as part of its struggle for equal citizenship in Victoria.

Much like the ACSC, the American G.I. Forum was primarily composed of working-class Mexican Americans. And like the ACSC it promoted higher education for Mexican American youth as a way of helping to create a new Mexican American middle class. Naturally, it maintained a focus on the plight of the underprivileged.

LULAC councils appear to have been motivated by aspirations similar to the ACSC before it. Council 4319 developed a strong focus on issues directly affecting the Mexican American populace and took the ACSC's early steps toward gender parity even further. But in contrast to the ACSC, Council 4319 contained a cross-class membership, which likely accounts for its primary emphasis on scholarship funding. It broadened its mission by focusing on issues that impacted the entire community.

The de León Club differed significantly from Victoria's other twentieth-century organizations because of its clear class identification. Members were college-educated professionals who sought to carve out a niche of respectability within the larger society and in the process identify themselves as being apart from working-class Mexican Americans and their organizations. Such an identity was not possible before the mid-1960s because the Mexican American middle class in Victoria had remained relatively small. The de León Club, then, was a product of its time, yet it never sought to turn its back on either the Spanish language or Mexican culture. Indeed, the club's cooperative venture with the University of Houston, Victoria, is evidence of its desire to promote an appreciation for Mexican American history and traditions among the white, mainstream community. Yet its exclusivity and class-composition indicate that the club has sought to gain acceptance by the Anglo middle class, primarily for altruistic purposes, rather than to end discrimination across class lines.

Certainly the Mexican Americans of Victoria have never been a single entity, with a single outlook or single set of goals. While there are clear similarities among the various groups, particularly in their desire to help foster the growth of a new Mexican American middle class as well as in their pervasive accommodationist attitude, specific objectives and strategies set them apart. Similar differences have shaped the divergent worldviews and actions of Mexican Americans in other Texas communities.

5
Strength through Adversity
Struggles for Political Inclusion

J UST AS Mexican Americans in Victoria employed fraternal organizations and sought educational equality to express and promote their views of citizenship, so too did they turn to political
action. Prior to World War II most Mexican Americans remained politically quiescent. Ongoing activity at the polls, on the stump and in
the courts, however, marked the post-1945 period. But the struggle was
never easy and Mexican Americans who sought to bring about significant political change in Victoria faced an Anglo-American establishment committed to the political exclusion of nonwhites. In the civic
realm, much as in that of fraternal associations and education, Mexican
Americans in Victoria supported the theoretical framework of American politics while questioning its discriminatory tendencies. Dedicated
to the basic economic and political structures of the nation as well
as popular conceptions of American democracy, Victoria's Mexican
American community sought to gain greater access to the voting booth
and to fair political representation through the Democratic Party. Mexican Americans considered themselves, for the most part, to be Democrats. Most opposed the conservatism advocated by the Republican
Party, though as the decades passed some found its party's message se-
ductive. This gradual movement into Republican Party ranks pointed
to increasing levels of diversity within the Mexican American com-

munity and to a slowly increasing tendency to have political interests driven by economics and ideology rather than by ethnicity.

PRIOR TO the 1950s the Mexican American vote in Texas had been a significant political factor only in limited areas along the border and in the machine-dominated politics of the southern portion of the state. Democratic Party bosses such as Manuel Bravo in Zapata County, Manuel Guerra in Starr County, James Wells in Cameron County, and Archer "Archie" Parr in Duval County influenced local politics relying on Mexican Americans as their electoral base.[1] Generally speaking, Mexican Americans did not engage in politics to a more consequential degree for numerous reasons. Until enforcement of the Voting Rights Act of 1965, many Mexican Americans were prevented from voting by Anglo society through exclusionary means. The most obvious example of such tactics was the poll tax. To Mexican Americans living on a shoestring budget, even the $1.50 charged in Victoria was prohibitive. Additionally, the act of registration was often an intimidating thought for many Mexican Americans who were already suspicious of Anglo institutions and authority figures. This widespread discomfort with Anglo society and a sense that the political system was not intended to serve Mexican American interests were perhaps the most significant factors limiting Mexican American political participation prior to the 1950s.[2]

Compounding things for Victoria's Mexican American community was the understanding that political activity was the domain of Anglo-Americans and that such a rule was not to be challenged. Many working-class Mexican Americans feared being fired by Anglo bosses for unpopular political activism. Thus intimidation by Anglo authority figures combined with the potential of material repercussions led the majority of Mexican Americans to recede into the barrio and to consider politics as the protected province of first-class citizens, that is: Anglo citizens.[3]

But the post–World War II period witnessed Mexican Americans reconsidering American politics. This changed attitude led to the appearance of several Mexican American political organizations in Victoria. The emergence of such organizations among Mexican Americans expressed evolving self-definitions of the group as equal American citizens who were now poised to assert their rights and their claim for public legitimacy.

The founding of the aforementioned American Citizens' Social Club in 1947 and its subsequent political activism helped bring Mexican Americans to the realization that they could, if they organized and worked together, have a voice in local politics. Thus poll tax drives in the 1950s and 1960s, led both by the ACSC and the AGIF, helped raise the consciousness of voting Mexican Americans.[4] Throughout these two decades, additionally, the ACSC, with its membership peaking in the mid-1960s at 700, forced politicians to at least make appearances and pay lip service to the interests of the Mexican American community.[5]

Groups such as the AGIF and the ACSC faced the challenge of struggling for political rights while simultaneously attempting to avoid being labeled as "leftists." This was especially troubling according to one scholar, "during the McCarthyite 1950s and later during the 1960s when reactionaries smeared civil rights activists with charges of radicalism."[6] Mexican Americans in Victoria recognized that winning elective office was more difficult and complex for their candidates than for their Anglo counterparts because minority nominees had to overcome a tradition of discrimination fueled by definitions of normative in ways that excluded them. Despite these obstacles they undertook campaigns to support Mexican Americans for political office. Such efforts to challenge exclusive definitions of citizenship always occurred through "proper" institutional channels and seldom opposed institutional or ideological structures. Mexican Americans simply wished to make these institutions more congruent with American ideals of democracy and republicanism and thereby more accessible and responsive. Ordinarily, Mexican American spokespersons in the city rejected out of hand radical ideas and tactics.

ACSC and AGIF efforts to engage Mexican American citizens politically led directly to the election of the aforementioned attorney Manuel Velasco to the VISD School Board in 1958.[7] Velasco was an attorney who had moved to Victoria in the mid-1950s. He was drawn to Victoria because of the reputation of the American Citizens' Social Club and his belief that the city held the potential to become an important center of political activity. Velasco's successful run for the school board in 1958 was both a stunning victory and a bitter disappointment. In one sense his election was a historic landmark. He was the first elected official in Victoria since the end of Mexican rule in

Clockwise from top left: Nick Hinojosa (first Mexican American county commissioner), John Artero (second Mexican American on VISD school board), Joe Peña (first Mexican American city councilman), and Martin Cano (followed Artero on the school board). *Courtesy* Pauline O. Peña

1836, and his success seemed to represent unlimited possibilities for future Mexican American involvement in government. In reality, however, his precedent did not signal the dawning of a new egalitarian age for Mexican American candidates in local politics so much as it marked a much smaller yet still significant and necessary milestone: he had achieved a measure of respectability reserved traditionally for whites. He had gained acceptance and become part of the norm with enough Anglo voters to secure a one-term stint on the school board. Velasco was able to achieve this success because of his position: the first Mexican American lawyer to practice in the city. As an educated professional he presented an air of respectability to the Anglo community.

His actions on the school board were relatively subdued in that he did not attempt to bring about new programs to benefit the poor or minority students. His platform and actions centered on the practical daily chores of hiring of teachers and deciding whether or not to charge students new fees for typing classes. While some might interpret Velasco's actions on the board as accommodative, in fact these were important steps toward gaining acceptance as citizens and marked a turning point in Victoria's political history. In reality Velasco could not have campaigned or served in any other way. For a Mexican American candidate to talk specifically about Mexican American issues at that time would have transformed such an individual from one interested in representing the entire community into one who spoke solely for a narrow constituency.[8]

In the 1950s officials ostensibly ran to represent the entire city. White politicians campaigned in the name of "the people" yet their actions benefited primarily the Anglo community. The fact was that according to accepted social conventions, white candidates, by virtue of controlling the economy, politics, and the cultural landscape, had created an environment in which they proffered themselves as the true keepers of the common good. The fact that white politicians who supported the racist status quo in reality voiced the needs of a narrow constituency was beside the point. It was accepted that Anglo candidates were capable of representing "all of the people." Since in the public consciousness American meant Anglo, so too did other descriptors such as "community," "the city," and "the county." When Anglo candidates stated an interest in the betterment of society, they never felt compelled to give assurances that their interests extended beyond the Anglo community.[9]

But in order to gain Anglo support Mexican Americans cooperatively had to emphasize their loyalty and sense of community responsibility regardless of how accomplished their past record may have been. Mexican American candidates had to prove that they were interested in the wider electorate, not solely their ethnic group. Velasco had been able to do that while also gaining the trust of AGIF and ACSC, which at this time were acting in concert to promote hitherto unprecedented levels of Mexican American voting activity. By drawing the majority of Mexican American votes and a small portion of the Anglo vote, Velasco was able to secure one term on the VISD School Board.[10] After Velasco's term ended two years later there would not be another Mexican American elected public official for another eight years.

Shortly after the end of his tenure on the school board in the summer of 1961 Velasco invited fifty Mexican American leaders to gather in Victoria, many from the 1960 Viva Kennedy clubs, to organize what he and his counterparts called the Mexican American Political Association (MAPA), an organization that they hoped to launch at a statewide level. The group pushed for the appointment of district judge J. E. D. Salinas of Laredo to fill the post of U.S. Judge for the Western District of Texas, which had been opened by the death of former governor James V. Allred. Texas's Mexican Americans claimed that the seat had been promised to them in return for their support of the Democratic political ticket in 1960. Out of the meeting Velasco earned election as the legal counsel of the group, and Oscar Phillips, also of the AGIF, was elected as chaplain.[11] Despite high hopes at the first meeting of MAPA, the group quickly dissolved as members were drawn to other organizations (such as the ACSC and the AGIF), and the leadership found it impossible to sustain the same missionary zeal that had originally brought them together.[12] Ultimately, the organization changed its name to the Political Association of Spanish Speaking Organizations (PASSO) and became an important force in other parts of the state where Mexican Americans tended to be even more activist.[13]

The next successful Mexican American candidate for office was John Artero, a local businessman also acceptable to Victoria's Anglo voters. Running on a platform that consciously avoided an emphasis on minority issues, Artero too, won enough Anglo support that when added to the Mexican American vote allowed him to win one term on the VISD Board in 1967. As with Velasco, Artero's term in office was distinguished by attention to issues such as the overall budget and the need for a new football stadium.[14]

Thus the period from 1945 to 1969 offered a mixed bag of political victory and stasis for Mexican Americans in Victoria. On the positive side two members of their community had managed to gain election to public office. Yet the basic political infrastructure that precluded a ticket of viable Mexican American candidates remained intact. The at-large voting system ensured that only Anglo candidates, or those very few Mexican Americans who were palatable to a large enough segment of the Anglo community, ever had a chance at election. Nonetheless during this period Mexican Americans in Victoria had sought to marshal the weaponry of citizenship to gain equality. The success of Velasco and Artero underscored the importance of the type of public legitimacy that could only be gained by the overt embracing of a middle-class identity. Their victories deepened the resolve of Victoria's Mexican American community to continue promoting education as the ticket to upward mobility, public validation, and political influence.

As the city entered the eighth decade of the century Mexican American youth began to question and challenge the status quo. While their ideas and actions never posed a realistic threat to Anglo-dominated politics, they did mark a temporary change in the political consciousness of at least one element within Victoria's Mexican American community. Over the next fifteen years Mexican American political activity in Victoria would be marked by a brief flirtation with the Chicano movement, and more substantively, by the emergence of a new cadre of viable political candidates. This impulse would be helped along by the national government that now intended to correct over a century of political injustice, by the growing public awareness of a nascent Mexican American professional class, and by an increased sense of political empowerment throughout the community.

The rise of the Chicano movement nationwide originally was reflected in a rather amorphous coincidental set of events that grew out of a sense of frustration with the status quo of the 1960s. Reies López Tijerina and his land reacquisition drive in New Mexico, farm worker efforts at unionizing in California led by César Chávez, Corky Gonzáles's initiative through the Crusade for Justice in Denver, along with activism among college campus organizations comprised a loosely connected movement. Only later did the Raza Unida Party (RUP) become a coalescing agent that drew these disparate groups and their leaders together in a common critique of American society and in a shared dedication to social and political reform.

There is still debate among scholars about the meaning of *el movimiento*. Historians generally tend to emphasize the differences between its participants and those belonging to the post–World War II G.I. generation. The G.I. generation was grounded in a patriotic culture that emphasized ways in which Mexican Americans could support fundamental economic and political principles in American society while bringing about evolutionary change. The Chicano generation, by contrast, sought a more revolutionary transformation that wrapped itself in Mexican culture and focused on a critique of American society. To be sure, the G.I. generation took pride in its Mexican history and culture as did the Mexican American generation before and the Chicano generation after it. Traditionally, Mexican American organizations such as LULAC had promoted the interests of Mexican American youth, but this primarily took the form of scholarships and summer youth recreation programs. It was not until the Chicano movement that young people achieved importance as activists and leaders. Shunning the actions and ideologies of organizations of the G.I. generation such as LULAC and the AGIF, which young people saw as being too gradualist and accommodative, Chicano youths employed a rhetoric of confrontation and separatism.

But it is too simplistic to dismiss G.I. generation activism as gradualist and Chicanismo as being hostile to American values and ideals. Even among Chicanos in Crystal City, the heart of the Raza Unida Party and Chicano political militance, there prevailed a strong degree of consensus in support of basic political tenets and a belief that opportunities for success did exist. Thus while young Crystal City Chicanos saw themselves as ethnically distinct from the American mainstream they had also developed a meaning of Americanism and embraced the notion that they belonged in this country. Additionally, the majority of them (bilingual and bicultural) believed that they had the same chance at success as anyone else if they only worked for it. This sense of Americanism involved a belief in the superiority of capitalism over other economic systems, particularly socialism, and a belief in American political traditions. They similarly accepted such values as the Protestant work ethic, honesty, education, responsibility, and egalitarianism that the dominant culture assumed to be inherently white.[15] Mexican Americans who embraced such ideals, according to the dominant mode of thought, had successfully been assimilated and taught to trade in their Mexicanidad for an American identity. For both the G.I. generation and Chicanos, however, such measures were understood to be part of the fabric of Mexican culture as well.

Although the Chicano movement was never widespread throughout Victoria's Mexican American community there nevertheless surfaced a small pocket of Chicanismo. Originally, discontented Chicanos had organized a local chapter of the Mexican American Youth Organization (MAYO) and lobbied local schools for Chicano literature in the libraries and engaged in grass-roots level political action. When school officials were unresponsive, militant Chicanos followed the example being set by their counterparts in other regions of the country and took to the streets, engaging in their own "blowout." [16]

On Wednesday, Diez y Seis de Septiembre (September 16), 1970, 150 Chicanos from Stroman High School, Victoria's south side and predominantly minority high school, walked out of classes and headed toward Victoria High School in the central portion of town; then they marched to Victoria College and returned to the Community Center across the street from Stroman High School. They chose September 16 because that was the day in 1810 when Father Miguel Hidalgo issued *el grito de Dolores* (the cry of Dolores) signaling the beginning of New Spain's war for independence against the Spanish. Later that afternoon the same students marched again from Stroman to the downtown area where they held a rally with various speakers. They sought to memorialize the death of Rubén Salazar, the Chicano journalist from Los Angeles who had been killed by police during the Chicano Moratorium earlier that year, and to protest the lack of attention given to Mexican American contributions to American history and society. Traditionally, they argued, Mexican Americans were rarely incorporated into the public school curriculum, and in those few instances, only in a negative light. The protesters were demonstrating to bring attention to this void in their education, to see that the schools drew various aspects of the Mexican American experience into the classroom, and to get libraries to stock Mexican American literature on their shelves. The protesters demanded the hiring of more Mexican American teachers and counselors in the VISD. Several of the speakers emphasized nonviolent resistance as ways of promoting *la causa*. [17]

The prime mover of the *huelga* (strike) at Stroman High School was Jimmy Rodríguez, a young Chicano from Victoria who was home on leave from Fort Bliss. Rodríguez and the other *huelgistas* won the support of Father Simone of Our Lady of Sorrows, the Mexican American Catholic church situated on the south side of town. Father Simone had taught parishioners that civil disobedience was justifiable in certain circumstances and was sympathetic to the concerns of the city's young Chicanos. His presence in the march added credibility to the students' demands and may have helped draw parental support, which would have been much more difficult to gain for such a bold action.[18]

Interestingly enough, no backlash occurred either in the short or long term. Amid prior rumors that violence would erupt at the demonstration the police had been called out but remained cool observers only. School administrators expelled no one. No students' parents were fired from their jobs. Local officials minimized the episode, concerned that over-publicizing the walkout might instigate further actions. The *Victoria Advocate* also downplayed events, at least compared to the coverage given them by the Corpus Christi *Caller Times*. While the *Caller Times* article focused on the speeches given at the rally and attempted to place the march in the context of social protest, the *Advocate* only gave the demonstration three sentences and buried the report in the back of the news section. The short article only mentioned that some students had "paraded through sections of the city Wednesday . . . apparently in celebration of Diez y Seis the anniversary date of Mexico's independence from Spain." The paper dutifully pretended as though nothing of any significance had happened in an apparent attempt to avoid publicizing the event, indicating, for instance that there had been one march rather than two.[19] For Victoria's city leaders (and the *Advocate*, the elite's mouthpiece) the tactic of nonresponse seemed to work. There were no further demonstrations anywhere in the city or in the schools, and MAYO itself stagnated and shortly thereafter disappeared. But the spirit of protest embodied by MAYO and the huelga continued to burn in the hearts of some Victoria Chicanos, and that momentum was transferred from MAYO to the RUP.

The Raza Unida Party in Texas emerged out of a Mexican American tradition of self-help when more formal, mainstream institutions ignored them.[20] Certainly Victoria's Chicanos believed very strongly that the "system" had indeed failed them, and thus turned to RUP as a political alternative. RUP was driven not only by a sense of indignation over decades of neglect and dismissal but also by a renaissance of pride in Mexican culture. MAYO had thus served as a conduit for transferring Mexican American cultural nationalism into support for the RUP.[21]

Led by Ramón Villa, Victoria's RUP became active in stirring support for Ramsey Muñiz, the party's candidate for Texas governor in 1972. During his first stop in Victoria, Muñiz spoke to a cheering crowd of 350 expressing to them a belief in an Americanism of a different kind, one of social justice and equality. "We would like to enjoy the fruits of Americanism that all other people enjoy," he stressed. Muñiz went on to proclaim that, "We don't mind being taxed with representation, but we don't like being taxed without representation." In this way Muñiz and the RUP were attempting to use the rhetoric of Americanism to develop a form of social criticism that would be palatable to Victoria listeners.[22] In other parts of the state, comparatively, Muñiz took a more militant public stance and attacked the Anglo-controlled political establishment. The RUP consisted of a delicate coalition of moderates and conservatives, liberals and radicals, and urban and rural forces, and so Muñiz and others perforce remained sensitive to the nature of their audiences. When MAYO organizer José Angel Gutiérrez appeared before an RUP gathering at the local Holiday Inn in October, 1972, for instance, he too echoed a message that encouraged Mexican Americans to take advantage of their rights as Americans and become politically active through the RUP.[23]

While the RUP in Victoria never fielded its own candidates for local office it did actively support statewide candidates, among them Muñiz who returned to the city in 1974 as he made another run for governor. This time around, Muñiz and the RUP followed a moderate strategy, attempting to appear less threatening to the establishment and more responsive to broader issues that went beyond the Mexican American community such as those affecting the poor. Muñiz told a Victoria crowd, for example, that he hoped to reform the state tax system, replacing the regressive sales tax with a tax on corporate profits.[24]

Despite the popular public support given to Muñiz and the RUP in Victoria and around the state in 1972 and 1974 most Mexican American voters continued to support the Democratic Party. In the 1972 election, for example, 61 percent of Mexican American voters statewide supported Dolph Briscoe, the Democratic candidate, while 6 percent voted for Republican Henry Grover, and only 33 percent of Mexican American voters cast ballots for RUP candidate Ramsey Muñiz. While the RUP vote was disappointingly small to Chicano activists, it was substantial enough to cause state Democrats to look at Chicano issues with more understanding. For the first time since Reconstruction — because of Muñiz' 6 percent showing in the overall state vote — Texas came very close to having a Republican governor in 1972.[25]

In Victoria, Muñiz that year received 1,221 votes against 6,150 for

Grover and 8,019 for Briscoe. Muñiz failed to win any voting precinct outright, managing a strong showing only in one precinct located in the heavily Mexican American southeast side of the city.[26] Ultimately, Muñiz captured just under 8 percent of the county vote in 1972, two percentage points higher than he took statewide. But this slight difference must be considered in a broader context. The higher percentage of votes taken by Muñiz in Victoria was less a reflection of Victoria's Mexican Americans' desires for drastic change than it was of growing discontent with both parties, particularly the Democratic Party, which had chosen conservative businessman Dolph Briscoe as its nominee. Indeed, when Muñiz ran for governor again two years later he only managed to get 4 percent of the county vote in an election that was marked by a pervasive sense of voter apathy as indicated by a total voter turnout that was two-thirds smaller than the 1972 showing.[27] Following Muñiz's arrest in 1975 for drug possession and the subsequent deterioration of the tenuous RUP coalition, Chicanos turned once again to the Democratic Party, which was now willing to be more receptive to Chicano concerns. The Democrats feared that even though the RUP was not likely to win any major elections it was still capable of playing the role of spoiler for Democratic candidates in an increasingly competitive two-party atmosphere.[28]

By the 1970s, then, Mexican Americans in Victoria were increasingly becoming political players. But one major obstacle remained: the ability to field winning candidates for office. In this respect the experience of Mexican Americans in Victoria mirrored that of Mexican Americans in other parts of the state. Even in areas with a predominance of Mexican Americans, such as El Paso, Mexican American candidates found it difficult to win political positions. From 1873 to 1980, for instance, despite its heavily Mexican American population, El Paso only had elected two Mexican American mayors. This state of affairs existed because Mexican American candidates in El Paso faced three obstacles: Mexican American poverty, "a cohesive Anglo business community, and a racially biased Anglo electorate."[29]

This situation differed little in Victoria. Contending with indigence precluded many Mexican Americans from taking an interest in something as esoteric as politics. Moreover, the ability of the tightly knit Anglo business community to lay out the terms of public debate along with widely diffused though generally unspoken ideas about the qualifications and ability of various candidates discouraged Mexican American participation. Further dissuading interest in political races was the notion that only Anglo candidates were capable of representing all citizens objectively. Yet despite the odds and the negative climate, increased numbers of Mexican American candidates began challenging the exclusive definition of citizenship by running for office in the early 1970s and beyond.

Among the first was Pete Cantú, owner of Cantú's Flower Shop, 2002 SW Ben Jordan, who in 1971 filed as a candidate to run for place four on the city council. Even though all the city council seats were elected at-large, each candidate had to file for a specific place. Cantú faced Roger Dawson and Sam Green Jr., but never made it past the primary. Although on the surface Cantú could have made a claim to worthiness by virtue of his business experience, he faced numerous handicaps. First, he was not connected with the city elite, Anglo or Mexican American. Thus he was not able to garner the kind of financial and verbal support necessary for victory. Moreover, he faced the common assumption that Mexican Americans were ill equipped to serve office. Further, he had no grass-roots organization behind him. Cantú won only one polling box, that at Hopkins School, a predominantly Mexican and African American site. Elsewhere, Cantú got dismal response. In southern voting boxes with mixed population, such as the Courthouse (downtown), Patti Welder Junior High School (south side), and Juan Linn Elementary (central Victoria), Cantú garnered between one-fourth and one-third of the balloting, while the majority of the remainder was split between his two Anglo opponents. In northern boxes Cantú never stood a chance. Stanly Elementary, tucked away in one of Victoria's older exclusive middle-class neighborhoods, gave Cantú less than 10 percent of its vote.[30]

In 1977 Hildo Luera, a local businessman,[31] contested Willis Armstrong for a place in the city council. Armstrong had several advantages in his favor: incumbency, and concomitantly, name recognition, and just as important in Victoria, the at-large election system. Luera faced the additional drawback of having a very ethnic sounding name, which he tried to play to his advantage by using radio advertising to ask and answer the question, "Who's Hildo?" Still working further against Luera was his refusal to request the endorsement of the local Anglo political elites. He intentionally avoided seeking such support for two reasons. First he was not interested in kowtowing to the self-appointed king-makers, and second, he realized that Armstrong, being a prominent member of the business community, would likely receive their support instead.[32]

Through the course of the doomed campaign Luera nonetheless developed a measure of backing among Anglo voters. He did so by adding a class dimension to the order of race relations in Victoria. He found blue-collar Anglos receptive to his working-class appeals and he courted their support. Luera lost in a close race but it marked the end of Armstrong's political career as he declined to run for reelection in the subsequent election cycle.[33] Despite the closeness of the contest it was obvious that the at-large voting system made it almost impossible for Mexican American candidates who rebuffed the support of leading local Anglo elites to win citywide elections.

Cantú's race, then, indicated that as late as the 1970s Mexican Americans remained disadvantaged and unrepresented in Victoria's political power structure. The dominant attitude that enforced such discriminatory political behavior simultaneously stifled advantages elsewhere, especially regarding issues where conservative, middle-class Anglos created a hostile public climate for Mexican Americans, among them the poor who needed uplifting. This was the case in an episode involving city council opposition to federal funding.

In a special meeting of the Victoria City Council held on May 22, 1978, the executive director of the Victoria Department of Community Affairs, Don Polzin, submitted an application for $11,820 in federal money to subsidize the Summer Youth Recreation Program. The Summer Youth Recreation Program was a federally funded project designed to provide field trips and other activities for children whose families received Aid to Families with Dependent Children (AFDC) funding. All the city had to do to secure the $11,820 was to indicate to the Community Services Administration that it needed the grant.[34]

But the city council opposed the funding, even though the money would not come out of local coffers. The council believed that the program would prove detrimental to local youths by exposing them to the foolishness of receiving something for nothing. Councilman R. E. Gene Hobbs, expressing concern over the moral development of Victoria's disadvantaged young people, argued that these youths should learn early in their lives that there is no free lunch. The Victoria Citizen's Advisory Committee (CAC) disagreed and lobbied passionately for approval of the program. Ed Warren, a member of the CAC's finance subcommittee, argued that resuming it was "the moral, ethical and proper thing to do."[35] While Warren and Charlie Steele, the Committee's finance subcommittee chairman, saw the program as beneficial to idle, impoverished young people, city council members branded the program as being philosophically unjustifiable. The mistrust of government and the myth of a living pioneer spirit shaped a conservative ideology that disallowed city council members from understanding the importance of such a program. Additionally, the ideology in opposition to the summer project helped conceal the fact that the majority of children who would benefit from it would be minority children. Polzin argued that the money paid for trips to the capitol building in Austin and to the Alamo as well as to other important historic places that these children would not normally get to visit. Thus the trips were educational in nature and not just for entertainment. But such logic fell on deaf ears.

The decision to reject the federal funding for the summer program raised the ire of the League of Women Voters (LWV), the NAACP, and LULAC. Speaking for the entire council, Assemblyman R. E. Hobbs said that he was "fed up with 100% giveaway programs."[36] Hobbs and fellow councilman James Coleman Jr. developed an alternative proposal in which children would have to pay a fee to participate or would have to perform work, presumably to "earn" the right to participate in the program. In making a case for his alternative project Hobbs said that the governmental program was "simply teaching those kids that there really is a free lunch."[37] The alternative proposal passed on a 3 to 1 vote with Hobbs and Coleman joined by Councilman Ted B. Reed (Councilman A. Willis Armstrong opposed).[38] But under public pressure from outraged minority citizens and women, the council later reversed itself and voted to accept the federal allotment. Councilman Reed argued that he had only opposed the measure earlier because he was concerned about the lack of accountability for the funds, but that he had since been provided an adequate explanation of how the money would be allocated and accounted for. Councilman Armstrong continued his support for the plan. Councilman Coleman, who had originally drawn up the alternative plan, changed his vote. All three were joined by Mayor C. C. Carsner who voted, even though not required to, in order to make his position public on the matter. Hobbes remained opposed to the whole idea.[39]

In voicing their support for the program Carsner and Armstrong still noted their displeasure for the government dole. Both believed that it was another example of unnecessary Washington, D.C., interference in local affairs and of liberal governmental waste of taxpayer money. Still smarting, Armstrong stated that the city should fight waste and make a stand for local control on "some other battleground."[40] Mayor Carsner, for his part, "criticized the federal government, and particularly the Department of Health, Education and Welfare which administers the program, for the cost of their services and for the hindrances those costs impose on the economy. But, he added, opposition to the local program would have little effect, so he, too, supported it."[41]

That groups of women and Mexican Americans could exert such pressure and force the city council to act against its will was indicative of the changing climate of Victoria politics. Individuals like Carsner, Armstrong, Coleman, and Reed had gained office by appealing to the very narrow constituency reflected in their conservative ideologies. But the dawning political reality was that increasingly, women and minorities were making their political voices heard. By couching support for the program in as benign a rhetoric as possible, council members hoped to walk the fine line between insulting a growing number of women and minority voters on the one hand and not representing the conservative constituency whose support they needed, electorally and in business, on the other. Indeed, change was in the air as the decade of the 1970s wound to a close. With the dawn of the Reagan era (1981–89), ironically enough, the City of Victoria was about to undergo an important restructuring thanks to a routine examination of the City Charter.

In early 1980 the City of Victoria appointed a panel to examine possible revisions to the city's Charter. The Charter Revision Committee led by mayor C. C. Carsner consisted of one African American male, one Mexican American female, two Mexican American males, and several Anglos: one retired school administrator, a banker, the president of the Victoria LWV, a businessman (and former city council member), and an insurance and real estate broker. Of the six Anglos, only one was somewhat sensitive to minority issues. And while the ethnic and racial composition appears fairly equitable the reality of the matter was that one of the Mexican American males was Wence de León. The only members of the group who held the potential for controversy were auto repair shop owner Alex Rojas and attorney Lydia Serrata Ledesma.[42] As things turned out, Lullis Jackson, the sole African American on the committee, also became a voice for change.

That February the LWV, the NAACP, the Mexican American Chamber of Commerce and LULAC called for the new charter to establish single-member districts (SMDs).[43] The LWV noted that of the twenty-four individuals who had served on the Victoria City Council in the prior twenty-three years, 26.5 percent were in business, 25 percent were professionals, 12.5 percent were industrial executives, 4 percent were in sales, and 4 percent were in supervisory positions, while 8 percent were public employees. The LWV report informed readers that over that time span, roughly three-fourths of all city council members had been drawn from a narrow segment of the population.[44] The Mexican American Chamber of Commerce further argued that at-large elections precluded gains by minority candidates. Since 1959, eight Mexican Americans had run for city council and all had lost.[45]

Table 1. Mexican American Candidates for City Council, 1959-1977.

Year	Candidate	Votes Received	Result
1959	Oscar Phillips	904	Lost
1961	Willie Galvan	548	Lost
1963	Jesse Cano	900	Lost
1971	Pete Cantú	891	Lost
1973	Alex Luna	992	Lost
1975	Alfredo Jaime	943	Lost
1975	Beatrice Ochoa	1,096	Lost
1977	Hildo Luera	2,017	Lost

Source: Recommendations for Charter Revision from the Mexican American Chamber of Commerce to the City's Charter Revision Committee. Charter Revision Committee Files, Office of the City Secretary.

Mayor C. C. Carsner believed the existing charter to be adequate and saw no need for alterations. He did, however, allow that the city council should be expanded to six seats and that each seat should represent one geographical district within the city, and further, that the Council members should reside in the district they represent. Carsner made the argument that each district could have direct representation (in the form of a resident on the council) but still maintain an at-large system. And while he did not say it, the implication was clear — such a system would ensure a council dominated by Anglo voters.[46]

Deliberations about proposed charter revisions became heated when the issue of reapportionment arose. Committee members Charles Hanley (a banker) and Willis Armstrong (owner of the local Mayflower Moving Company franchise) expressed consternation fearing that if the committee could not devise something acceptable to minority representatives legal action would ensue.[47] Wence de León thus proposed a compromise that still allowed Anglo voters control of a majority of the city council. The revised plan called for three single-member districts and three seats and the mayor to be elected at-large. Alex Rojas strongly objected to the proposition as inadequate to minority concerns. Rojas countered that all council seats were to derive from single-member districts, although he showed inclination to support an alternative offered by attorney Lydia Serrata Ledesma that called for four single-member districts and the mayor and two council seats to be elected at-large.[48] In the end, de León's watered-down version won out with support from the Anglo members of the committee. His was the only viable alternative, de León argued, because aside from proportional representation another important task for the committee was "coming up with a plan that the majority of the people will approve."[49] De León's blueprint was then forwarded for approval by the city council, from which point it went before and was endorsed by the voters.[50]

The creation of even three SMDs marked one of the most significant leaps forward for the Mexican American electorate in Victoria and led to the election of Joe Peña, a postal employee, to the city council in 1981. Peña then remained in office until he stepped down in 1991. Through the coming years he proved to be an important voice for Mexican American interests. In June of 1988, for example, one Carlos Padilla, a resident of the south side of the city, called the city to ask that the gutters on his street be cleaned out. Two weeks later he still had not received a response by the city. Padilla called and spoke to Erskine Kleiber (superintendent of the street department) who, Padilla claimed, had hung up on him. While other city officials continued to stonewall any action, Councilman Peña informed his colleagues that he had checked the street in question and had noticed "a lot of dirt and garbage" along the curbs (he simultaneously publicly aired Kleiber's rude treatment of Padilla).[51] Within a brief period of time thereafter the city attended to the problem of unattended gutters. Although a rather mild issue, the incident and the way Peña handled it signified the ways in which Mexican Americans, now with SMDs and attendant electoral success, could exert influence upon governmental institutions in hitherto impossible ways.

While the city moved toward single-member districts in the 1980s, the county had not dealt with the question of district representation because of the existence of precincts. Each precinct elected one of its own residents to serve on the county commissioners' court. Given the changing face of politics in Victoria, Mexican Americans also decided to test the political waters at the county level. In 1980, Nick Hinojosa, owner of a small grocery store on the southeast end of the city, did just that. Hinojosa had moved to Victoria in the 1960s from Corpus Christi, Texas, seeking a smaller town in which to raise his family and find better work opportunities. In his capacity as storeowner he interacted closely with some of the city's most impoverished and powerless residents. Over the years he developed increasing levels of concern for the issues that plagued working-class Mexican Americans. And so he decided to try to rectify matters. He ran a well-organized campaign on a tight budget. But by knocking on doors and rallying Mexican American support he managed to win an upset victory over incumbent Herman Pargac in the Democratic primary. Riding the momentum of the primary victory, Hinojosa managed to win the general election, thereby making history by becoming the first Mexican American to serve on the commissioners' court.

Of importance had been his campaign rhetoric that appealed to "the people." "I was not running as a Mexican American. I said that from the beginning. I think it is important to represent everyone and to do what is best for the county and the precinct."[52] By adopting a broad platform he had garnered a significant following among Anglos. In none of the six voting places in his precinct was the vote even close.

Making the win even more impressive was the fact that once Hinojosa had defeated the incumbent Herman Pargac in the spring primary, two Anglo write-in Republican candidates appeared on the ballot hoping to waylay him. But again Hinojosa polled significantly more votes in every polling place in the precinct than the other two candidates combined.[53]

Nevertheless, voting patterns show that this landmark victory did not indicate a complete turnaround in the consciousness of Victoria's Anglo voters. The rural vote went to Hinojosa by slightly more than 2 to 1. Yet in the urban places, the margin of victory was just under 10 to 1. Rural voters tended to be Anglo, conservative, and not moved with the idea of helping to change social relationships by supporting a nonwhite candidate.

Hinojosa's victory in his run for county commissioner in 1980 was significant as it opened the eyes of Victoria Mexican Americans to the possibility that a minority candidate could indeed be elected to represent a precinct. Once in office he became very highly regarded among Mexican and Anglo-American officials and voters.[54]

In December, 1987, Frank J. Targac of Bloomington and Guthrie Sklar of Victoria filed as candidates for Victoria County Commissioner for Precinct 1 in the upcoming March 8 Democratic primary. Both hoped to overthrow two-term incumbent Nick Hinojosa. Their work was cut out for them as Hinojosa, the first Mexican American county commissioner in Victoria's history, had beaten the odds eight years earlier by defeating an Anglo incumbent. During his tenure in office he had developed a reputation as a powerful candidate and effective commissioner.[55]

But Targac turned out the winner in the primary, pulling off a stunning upset of Hinojosa by eighty-three votes. The urban polling sites for Precinct 1, which were in the south side of the city, went for Hinojosa. Targac, by contrast, won the rural polling places where a larger pool of Anglo voters resided. In the end Hinojosa supporters may have taken his presence in office, after two consecutive terms, for granted.[56]

Although the Victoria County precinct's structure had allowed for Mexican American political successes (as in the case of Hinojosa) the precinct system still tended to discriminate. In October of 1979, therefore, MALDEF and the Southwest Voter Research and Educational Project (SWVREP) filed suit against Victoria County because the precincts, as presently arranged, violated the principle of "one man one vote." Under the old arrangement voters in thinly populated areas carried considerably more institutional clout than voters in heavily populated precincts, which tended to be urban and were more likely to have a larger number of minority residents. While there were still Anglos and Mexican Americans in rural precincts, the majority of people living in the countryside were Anglo farmers and ranchers.[57]

In May of 1980 MALDEF and SWVREP lawyers asked U.S. district judge Owen D. Cox to nullify the results of the primary elections in Refugio and Victoria counties. In January, Cox had found apportionment in both counties as violating the principle of "one man one vote." But he gave the counties until June 1, 1981, to redraw precinct lines. He did not seek immediate reapportionment because he believed that it might prove too disruptive for the upcoming spring primaries. But MALDEF and SWVREP attorneys argued that the Fifth Circuit Court of Appeals in New Orleans, Louisiana, had recently ordered Harrison County, Texas, to redraw voting lines immediately. Therefore, so the lawyers argued, precedent had been set to institute immediate changes.[58]

Ultimately, no immediate action was taken. But as of March 6, 1982, Victoria County still had not submitted a reapportionment plan, in accordance with the Voting Rights Act of 1965, that the Justice Department found suitable. Thus MALDEF and SWVREP filed suit on March 5, 1982, in federal court asking that the justices implement an apportionment plan of their own. MALDEF and SWVREP offered their own suggested apportionment design that would have given minority voters a majority in at least two of the four county commissioner precincts.[59] On September 21, 1984, the commissioners' court approved voting precinct changes, as suggested by MALDEF, to become effective on March 1, 1985.[60]

But redistricting hardly changed old questions about Mexican American fitness for office, as became obvious in the Beatríz Quintanilla González and Juan Velásquez cases. On December 13, 1985, Victoria County Commissioners Court, behind the recommendation of then commissioner Nick Hinojosa, named local attorney Beatríz Quintanilla González to the post of Justice of the Peace for County Precinct 1. González was chosen out of a field of four Anglo male candidates and the widow of the deceased judge to replace Judge Alfred Baass, who had passed away the previous month. Commissioners chose González with only one abstention, that by Commissioner Jerry Nobles who supported Mrs. Baass.[61] Then, in 1986 González announced that she would formally run for election to the post of Justice of the Peace Precinct 1 in the upcoming May primary. "I know I am well qualified to serve as justice of the peace, and if elected I know I will continue to do a good job for all citizens who come into my court." Despite the fact that González lived in a predominantly Mexican American precinct she still felt obligated to emphasize her ability to do justice for all citizens out of both a sense of moral responsibility and political reality.[62] González emerged victorious but in the process she had to prove herself as part of the norm, as one of "the people."[63] In contrast, the other successful candidates running that same election season (Helen Walker for County Treasurer, Jerry Garrett for Judge of the Victoria County Court-at-Law #1, and Val D. Huvar for reelection, also for post of County Clerk) were all Anglo. As such, these candidates had the luxury of being immediately identified as part of the mainstream and therefore focused on specific issues without having to affirm their qualifications.

Not even incumbency was enough to confirm a person's ability to serve "all the people," however. When Juan Velázquez III ran for reelection to County Court-at-Law #2 in 1986 he found that ethnicity and its implications for the acceptability of a candidate mitigated the value of incumbency. Velásquez focused his campaign on changes he had brought about as judge (reducing the backlog of cases, implementing a program to provide restitution to crime victims, etc.). Nevertheless, Velásquez had to wait until all votes were counted late on election day to find out that he had indeed squeaked out a narrow victory. His opponent, Republican Eric Samuelson, was a virtual unknown, while Velásquez as incumbent had a reasonable amount of name recognition. Yet incumbency was almost not enough to reelect Velásquez.[64]

Party loyalty may have played an important role in keeping Velásquez in office, for by the 1980s in Texas, the growth of the Republican party had shifted the parameters of political debate. While conservative/liberal, or Anglo/Mexican issues had traditionally been played out within the philosophical understandings of the Democratic Party, the emergence of an increasingly viable Republican Party spelled a major shift so that ideological, gender, and ethnic battles began to reflect party lines. Thus the same conservative male Anglo element, which in the past would have worked to defeat Velásquez, now split in the primary between conservatives who remained in the Democratic Party and those who bolted for the Republican camp. Hence, rather than fighting out such battles in the primaries, the general election had become the main contest arena. Examination of the election returns bears out the ethnic and ideological splits in the county. Had Velásquez simply won a majority in all voting precincts, one could fairly surmise a generally pervasive measure of support for him. But the returns reflected a more complex scenario. Velásquez lost in rural precincts and those in the wealthier, more conservative, Anglo urban precincts.[65]

By contrast, Jerry Nobles had little difficulty winning his own race. Early on Nobles announced that he was running for reelection to County Commissioner Precinct 2, but as a Republican this time. He switched parties because of his conservatism. Nobles said, "In my opinion, the voters want people in public office who will look for ways to reduce spending rather than ones who look for ways to raise more taxes." This remark was a thinly veiled reference to white voters that drew on widespread stereotypes about "tax and spend" liberals whose welfare state benefited lazy minorities. Further, Nobles's comment fed into a growing anti-tax mood (one symptomatic of a conservative resurgence) that had been more prevalent among white than minority voters.[66]

As the Mexican American middle class evolved across the United States, particularly in the 1980s, some of the new professionals that constituted it also began to vote conservative Republican and became party activists. Actually, the middle class, broadly defined, includes small businessmen and other white-collar workers, and these segments of the Mexican American community have tended to remain in the Democratic Party. The neoconservatism that has been expressed among Mexican Americans has stemmed from a new generation of professionals: doctors, lawyers, CPAs, and engineers.[67]

Hildo Luera, who had run unsuccessfully for city council in 1977, was one of the more prominent Mexican American professionals to move toward the Republican Party in the 1980s. For Luera the decision involved more than simply economics and conservative ideology. Luera had attempted to be involved in Democratic Party politics earlier but had received a cold shoulder from the Democratic leadership. Because he felt that the Democratic Party, locally, was not responsive to Mexican Americans or Mexican American issues, he switched to the Republican Party wherein he found a more supportive climate. The Republican Party was simultaneously attempting to broaden its base, having been the traditional minority party in the city, county, and the state. It now countenanced higher levels of participation from activists like Luera. While the Democratic Party on the state and national levels played to Mexican American interests, the local party was more recalcitrant, having been dominated by the Anglo business elite.[68] Even in the 1980s it was still possible to be very conservative in Texas and be called a Democrat.

In 1984 Luera formed the Victoria County Hispanics for Reagan-Bush Committee. In announcing the organization's inception at a press conference, Luera stated that "the time has come for Hispanics to get involved" in politics. The small group that constituted the committee believed that the Democratic Party no longer served the interests of the Hispanic community. Invoking popular Republican Party rhetoric, Luera argued that Victoria's Hispanics had been driven into the Republican ranks because of Mexican American concerns with such issues as immigration reform and the right to work "without being under the thumb of big labor." Republican state senator J. E. "Buster" Brown, who also attended the press conference, noted how the Republican platform reflected "traditional Hispanic beliefs — pro-family, pro–freedom of religion, pro a viable work ethic." [69]

The creation of the Reagan-Bush committee reflected the new mood of the 1980s proclaiming Republican Party endorsement. Although a mass exodus of Mexican American voters did not occur overnight, small defections like Luera's pointed toward the reconsideration of old politics. Luera was a very successful local businessman, and like other conservatives, saw the Democratic Party as threatening to the traditional fabric of American life. That this accusation was untrue did not seem to matter.

Despite the many victories and progress of the 1980s, Mexican Americans as a group still found it hard to make concrete political headway in Victoria. They faced old-time conservatism and entrenched prejudice. When Rene Torres sought the Democratic nomination for District 32 in the Texas legislature in 1987 he held little chance of winning. He lost to his Democratic opponent in the primaries, who then went on to defeat against the Republican Steve Holzheauser in the general election.[70] Holzheauser's victory indicated that Republicans in Victoria County had emerged as a powerful political force. The anti-tax, anti–big government, culturally conservative rhetoric of Republican candidates had found a new base in Victoria and marked the beginning of a period of difficulty for Democratic candidates who were increasingly painted (fairly or not) as typical "tax and spend" liberals.

In the spring of 1989 Gil Gonzales decided to challenge incumbent Gary Breech for one of the two at-large city council positions. His campaign centered on the most pressing public policy issue at the time: the need for a new municipal water source. While Gonzales ran a race that pushed ethnicity to the background, the power of incumbency and a racially split citywide vote dictated that there would be no change in the status quo. Breech won handily by almost a 2 to 1 margin. The vote clearly reflected the reality that Victorians were still voting along racial lines. While there may have been some Mexican Americans who voted for Breech, and some Anglos may have pulled Gonzales's lever, predominantly Anglo precincts went to Breech, while mainly Mexican American areas backed Gonzales.[71]

THE EFFORTS launched by organizations such as the ACSC, the AGIF, and later LULAC to inspire Mexican American political participation were all undertaken in the spirit of consensualism. All three groups sought conformity and all pursued their ends within proper mainstream channels. Their accomplishments were mixed. While their initiatives increased the number of Mexican American registered voters, their efforts did not produce dramatic changes in the local balance of political power. On the more positive side they raised the consciousness of Mexican Americans about political activity. The ACSC, the AGIF, and LULAC further helped swell the ranks of the Democratic Party, which Mexican Americans saw as best serving their interests.

One key aspect of the Democratic Party has been its focus on the role of the state, but until the World War II era Mexican Americans saw the state to be in collusion with Anglo-Americans intending to oppress them. Hence Mexican Americans looked with suspicion at political institutions. Even the act of registering and voting induced feelings of apprehension. As American Citizens' Social Club ex-president Matt López noted, "people were afraid . . . they were afraid of going in that little box and voting."[72] However, due to the growing sense of American nationalism sparked by the two world wars, the New Deal, and the civil rights movement, a significant segment of the Mexican American community began to think of the state as a vehicle for self-improvement, a means to help mitigate the negative effects of over a century of nativist racism that had resulted in their second-class citizenship. As a result, Mexican American Democrats looked to the ballot box and to government as an ally and began turning toward the judiciary to overcome traditions of unfair political practices. Hence there came to be a portion of the community that believed the courts were the friends of Mexican American struggles for citizenship.

But at the same time the incipient Mexican American middle class in Victoria saw the state as detrimental to their overall interests. Thus occurred something with possibly long-lasting implications in Victoria's politics: the emergence of a viable Mexican American wing of the Republican Party. Throughout the 1970s and beyond, the growing middle and professional class began defining its political interests as much in class terms as ethnic ones. While this element did not, as a whole, turn its back on Mexican heritage and culture, economic conservatism combined with traditionally conservative cultural perspectives attracted increasing numbers within the middle-class ranks to the Republican Party. The drastic turn of the Democratic Party to the left following the 1968 national convention, the subsequent disastrous presidential nominations of George McGovern, Walter Mondale, and Michael Dukakis, along with growing control of the Democratic Party by what Republicans labeled as "dangerous liberalism" made the rhetoric of individualism, limiting governmental interference with business, "family values," and American international power seem very attractive indeed.

Equality within U.S. society, then, has been the quest of Mexican Americans in Victoria. Change has always been pursued through means already in place, especially those offered by the Democratic and Republican parties. Ethnicity, which mainstream America finds threatening at times, is not something they have injected into local politics, though Mexican Americans have never denied their heritage. Hispanic communities elsewhere have taken a similarly moderate path.

Conclusion

VICTORIA'S Mexican American history appears to be a departure from the standard historiography on Tejano communities that argues that a questioning of mainstream institutional life and confrontational tactics were the norm, particularly during the 1960s and after. Historians who have researched twentieth-century communities such as Los Angeles, Houston, San Antonio, and El Paso have noted how people therein engaged in an array of tactics — among them founding civic leagues, organizing exploited laborers, and even leveling criticism at police forces — to make Anglo society responsive to Mexican American rights as citizens. The Chicano movement of the 1960s and 1970s was part of a phase in this ongoing struggle for recognition. The ethnic politics of recent decades still employ a confrontational rhetoric that is in keeping with approaches of days gone by.

In Victoria, in contrast, definitions of citizenship and a general consensual belief in the essential value of the American experiment in republican democracy together remained the most powerful and ubiquitous factors shaping relations between Mexican Americans and Anglos. Indeed, consensualism and widely accepted notions of normative goals and behavior as defined by the dominant culture were the unspoken, unnamed forces that drew Anglos and Mexicans together and allowed for peaceful negotiation.

Organizations representing Mexican American working-class and middle-class segments of the Mexican American community did not emerge in Victoria until after World War II, but even they can hardly be considered as ones calling mainstream institutions into question. At the core both working-class and middle-class organizations concentrated largely on educational issues in hopes of helping Mexican American youths achieve professional-class status. Thus people seldom reproached the fundamental nature and structure of Victorian or American societies. Rather, they developed a critique of the ways in which those societies treated Mexican Americans. The organizations and individuals discussed in this work rarely challenged the ideology under which existing social, political, and economic systems were premised but sought instead to forge a niche for Mexican Americans within them and to broaden the capacity for their inclusion.

This tendency to trust mainstream institutions, and to accept conservative, supposedly middle-class values has been evident ever since Mexican Americans began to run for public office, Mexican American organizations became increasingly involved in community affairs, and when Mexican Americans won seats on appointive boards by the 1970s. This increased public presence had been achieved without militancy on the part of Mexican Americans and indicated at least limited acceptance on the part of Anglos of a measure of Mexican American public participation (socially and politically). Hence while it could not be claimed that Mexican Americans had achieved anything approaching complete equality by the end of the twentieth century, certainly there had been positive strides.

The growth of the Mexican American professional class in more recent decades has contributed to the further entrenchment of the consensual order. Despite upward progress, successful elements in Victoria still abided by traditional (and conservative) Mexican American values such as the primacy of the family, the household patriarch, and Catholicism. While Victoria's Mexican Americans had assimilated in terms of political, economic, and to a degree social ideology, few lost touch with revered aspects of in-group homeland values. Historically, ethnic pride and identity informed the Mexican American community and a healthy chauvinism for Mexican culture always pervaded the city's Mexican American populace. Even the Catholic youth (many of whom did not speak Spanish) that became involved in the CYO Ballet

Folklorico recaptured a lost respect for their heritage. Cultural attachment to the old was always delicately balanced with a sociopolitical allegiance with Americanism, therefore. It was the tempering effect of this dual identity structure within the Mexican American community that further muted potential radicalism, certainly from the expanding professional classes.

Thus over time in Victoria there have been few examples of behavior remotely resembling militancy or inflammatory campaigns against discrimination. Except for the Amalgamated Clothing Workers of America, unions in the city and the Golden Crescent never emerged among businesses that relied primarily on Mexican American labor. Local clubs, societies, and organizations avoided open conflict with city, county, and school authorities. National groups such as LULAC and the AGIF repudiated any semblance of militancy or radicalism, even when they confronted discrimination directly. Mirroring this approach, local branches of these organizations challenged discrimination subtly, instead promoting schooling for young people hoping that someday education would negate the need for lawsuits or investigations to overturn discrimination.

Does Victoria's historical experience stand out as anomalous then? Were Victoria's Mexican Americans truly accommodationist? Did they lack *ganas* (desire)? The examples given here seem to confirm such an observation. But it is important to note that the temptation to emphasize Victoria's exceptionalism would be incorrect. The supposed middle-class consciousness (among a heavily working-class community) that so much permeated Victoria's Mexican Americans and cut across class and gender lines also played a significant role outside Victoria. The AGIF and LULAC, for instance, have traditionally embraced middle-class approaches and mainstream American political ideology. Neither group ever mounted serious critiques of capitalism or of the American political system. The role they played in the Mexican American civil rights struggle was always that of the loyal opposition. Their weaponry has traditionally been (with some exceptions) that of patriotic citizens: the vote, political action, and the judiciary.

Quiescence, therefore, may be too strong of a description for Victoria's Mexican American population. Since the settlement's early years during the 1820s, Victorians were keen of their secondary status in a racist society. The manner by which Mexican Americans in Victoria challenged the way they had been marginalized and excluded from American beneficence was through institutional avenues, the very model utilized by other disfranchised groups in American politics. Such approaches can hardly be categorized as unconventional in the American milieu. Indeed, the history of Mexican Americans in Victoria likely reflects the experiences of many other Texas Mexican American communities than has previously been conceded.

Notes

Introduction

1. Carlos Solís, interview with the author, May 1, 1996.

2. Ignacio García makes a similar point when he writes that Mexican American activists in the early 1960s had become "Americans who happened to be *mexicanos.*" Ignacio García, *Viva Kennedy: Mexican Americans in Search of Camelot*, 8. Also see Benjamin Johnson, *Revolution in Texas*, who traces this process of "Americanization" back to the 1910s.

3. This argument is not completely new. Ignacio García finds an accommodationist tone to post–World War II Mexican American activism in "Backwards from Aztlán: Politics in the Age of Hispanics," in Roberto M. De Anda, ed. *Chicanas and Chicanos in Contemporary Society*, 194. This work, however, digs more deeply into such a worldview at the local level and argues that it was less "accommodationist" than current literature allows.

4. I take the phrase from Peter N. Carroll's book about the United States in the 1970s, *It Seemed Like Nothing Happened: America in the 1970s*. In similar ways, we both argue that while on the surface it may appear that Victoria's Mexican Americans, or Americans in general in the 1970s, were passive, docile, and inactive, a deeper look shows how activists were working in new ways to organize resistance to the status quo. Carroll's and my arguments both stress the fact that this type of seemingly quiet, almost nonexistent activism was actually quite important with perhaps broader, long-range implications for policy and politics than the visible, overt activism of the 1960s.

5. In my attempts to redirect scholarly lines of inquiry, however, I do not mean to argue that Victoria was devoid of racism. Indeed, the case is made consistently throughout the work that Victoria has historically been a hostile environment for Mexican Americans; a situation they never wished to tolerate. The difference in Victoria was that the conflict that resulted from Mexican American resistance to racism took subtler forms. Mexican American Victorians saw cooperation as a usable alternative for contesting definitions of citizenship and challenging racist norms.

6. Armando Navarro, *The Cristal Experiment: A Chicano Struggle for Community Control.*

7. Ibid., 21.

8. Alex Saragoza, "Recent Chicano Historiography."

9. See for example, Mario T. García, *Mexican Americans: Leadership, Ideology, and Identity, 1930–1960*, and *Desert Immigrants: The Mexicans of El Paso, 1880–1920*.

10. See Noel Ignatiev, *How the Irish Became White*; Stefano Luconi, *From Paesani to White Ethnics*. For a discussion of how whiteness became a touchstone of citizenship in various forms in the nineteenth century see Alexander Saxton, *The Rise and Fall of the White Republic: Class Politics and Mass Culture in Nineteenth-Century America*. See also David Roediger, *The Wages of Whiteness: Race and the Making of the American Working Class*, for an examination of the ways in which the concept of whiteness was embraced and employed by the American working class to define itself and protect its threatened social status. Neil Foley's *The White Scourge: Mexicans, Blacks, and Poor Whites in Texas Cotton Culture*, examines the ways in which Texans created gradations of whiteness. Greater levels of whiteness allowed increased levels of access to economic success and social acceptance. My work is neither concerned with thoroughly theorizing whiteness nor demonstrating whether or not Mexican Americans sought to be defined in such terms. Rather, I focus on the ways in which Mexican Americans sought to negotiate fundamental assumptions about citizenship, which, whether publicly articulated or not, were based on notions of whiteness.

11. Ignacio García, *Viva Kennedy*, 6.

12. This is a theme echoed in ibid., 17. Here García argues that political participation in the early 1960s became the new avenue for political expression.

Chapter 1

1. Robert Shook, *Reflections of Old Victoria*, ix.

2. Ana Carolina Castillo Crimm, "Success in Adversity: The Mexican Americans of Victoria County, Texas, 1800–1880," 90. David Urbano, "The Saga of a Revolutionary Family: The Martín de León Family of Texas," 1–19.

3. Crimm, "Success in Adversity," 102. Also see Booth Mooney, *75 Years in Victoria*, 11.

4. Urbano argues that there were forty-seven families in Guadalupe Victoria. See Urbano, "Saga of a Revolutionary Family," 19.

5. Urbano, "Saga of a Revolutionary Family," 33.

6. John J. Linn, *Reminiscences of 50 Years in Texas*, 22.

7. Urbano, "Saga of a Revolutionary Family," 45.

8. Linn, *Reminiscences*, 36–41. Martín de León, founder of Guadalupe Victoria, succumbed in 1833 to a cholera epidemic.

9. Roy Grimes, *300 Years in Victoria County*, 134–35.

10. A. B. J. Hammett, *The Empresario: Don Martín de León*, 69.

11. Hammett, *Empresario*, 55.

12. Urbano, "Saga of a Revolutionary Family," 72. Also see Linn, *Reminiscences*, 322.

13. Hammett, *Empresario*, 58–59.

14. Urbano, "Saga of a Revolutionary Family," 61, 83, 92.

15. Crimm, "Success in Adversity," 179, 197.

16. Ibid., 185–86.

17. Ibid., 216–17.

18. Ibid., 202.

19. The "Black Legend" has its roots in historic tensions between the Spanish and British. Religious bigotry and overseas competition fueled British stereotypes of Spanish being vicious, barbarous, and greedy. When the hated Spanish mixed with Native Americans, the resulting mestizo (mixture of Spanish and Indian blood) was seen as a combination of barbarous, treacherous Spanish blood with the inferior, backward vicious Indian blood. Thus the result was a new breed of human that combined the worst traits of both races. The Black Legend encompassed not just a nationalistic component but also a religious, anti-Catholic one as well. For a full discussion of the roots of the Black Legend (*leyenda negra*) see Arnoldo De León's *They Called Them Greasers*, 63–74. Also see David J. Weber, *Foreigners in Their Native Land: Historical Roots of the Mexican Americans*, 68–71, and Urbano, "Saga of a Revolutionary Family," 58.

20. Sam W. Haynes, *Soldiers of Misfortune: The Somervell and Mier Expeditions; Victoria Advocate*, Historical Edition, May 2, 1968.

21. J. Frank Dobie, *Longhorns*, 27–28.

22. Linn, *Reminiscences*, 322–24.

23. Ibid., 322–24.

24. Frederick Law Olmsted, *Journey through Texas: Or a Saddle Trip on the Southwestern Frontier*, 245.

25. Olmsted, *Journey through Texas*, 235.

26. Hobart Huson, *Refugio: A Comprehensive History of Refugio County from Aboriginal Times to 1955*, II, 206–12. See also Ron Tyler et al., eds. *The New Handbook of Texas*, IV, 873–74; San Antonio *Express*, June 12, 1874, 2; June 13, 1874, 2; June 16, 1874, 2; J. Frank Dobie, A *Vaquero of the Brush Country*, 76.

27. Dobie, *Vaquero*, 76–78.

28. Mooney, *75 Years in Victoria*, 4.

29. Shook, *Reflections*, xiii; Penny Anderson et al., eds., *The Handbook of Victoria County*, 128–29.

30. Anderson, *Handbook of Victoria County*, 89–90.

31. Ibid., 72–73; Shook, *Reflections*, xiv.

32. Anderson, *Handbook of Victoria County*, 55.

33. Shook, *Reflections*, 9; *Victoria Advocate*, 88th Anniversary Issue, 1846–1934, 15.

34. *Victoria Advocate*, 88th Anniversary Issue, 1846–1934, 9, 13; Shook, *Reflections*, xiii; Anderson, *Handbook of Victoria County*, 49–50.

35. Anderson, *Handbook of Victoria County*, 129.

36. Crimm, "Success in Adversity," 268.

37. Interestingly enough, certain sections of the south side have remained the province of the Anglo upper class. Parts of the downtown area, and other portions of the city bounded by Riverside Park, Moody Street, Rio Grande, and Main Street are the sites of historic monumental mansions that are a testament not only to the wealth of the local elites but also to the staying power of tradition and conservatism.

38. *Victoria City Directory*, 1900–01.

39. United States Bureau of the Census, 1920, manuscript census at Victoria Public Library (hereafter VPL).

40. Lawrence Cardoso, *Mexican Emigration to the United States, 1897–1930: Socio-Economic Patterns*, 21–22. For more on commonly accepted stereotypes about Mexicans in Texas see De León, *They Called Them Greasers*.

41. Mark Reisler, *By the Sweat of Their Brow: Mexican Immigrant Labor in the United States, 1900–1940*, 157–58. Over time (as will be noted in chapter 2) the Catholic Church grudgingly came to accept Mexican Catholics, but first as a foreign group in need of Americanization. Only after the 1960s did the Catholic Church begin to see value in allowing Mexican Americans to retain aspects of their culture in worship rituals. For a more detailed discussion of the ideological underpinnings of nativism see John Higham's *Strangers in the Land: Patterns of American Nativism*.

42. "Sixty Years of Germany in America," Victoria Council of Defense, n.d., 6, 8, Texas State Archives, Austin, Texas, Good Neighbor Commission (hereafter GNC) Discrimination Files.

43. "Sixty Years of Germany in America," 2–5, Texas State Archives, GNC. In his explanation for the rejection of the request, Chairman of the Publicity Committee V. B. Proctor cited the opening words of the German national hymn: "Where is the German Fatherland? As far as the German tongue is spoken and German prayer is said." In this tract Proctor warned of the specter of "Pan-Germanism with its hideous gargoyles of dual allegiance and hyphenated citizenship." Proctor went on to add that, "If there are any people in Victoria County today that are going to conceive, suddenly or gradually, any sympathy for anything German, language or otherwise, the quicker they are smoked out of their holes the better it will be for the public welfare." Granted these statements were made in the heat of a worldwide conflagration, yet they indicated an important aspect of citizenship: the immigrant citizen candidate must be willing to relinquish most, or all vestiges of the homeland's culture. This was a sacrifice, so it appeared to Anglo-Americans, that was fair and that their predecessors had made.

44. Carole E. Christian, "Joining the American Mainstream: Texas's Mexican Americans during World War I," 559–60, 583–85, 587–90; and Mario T. García, *Mexican Americans*, 28.

45. *Victoria City Directory, 1933*.

46. Ironically, the entire complex was sold in the 1970s to Manuel Villafranca, who renamed the dance hall Club Westerner, and used it to attract a wide variety of Tejano music artists. Thus Villafranca's club has been a hotspot for Tejano music since the 1970s.

47. "A Fete Rain Couldn't Spoil," *Victoria Advocate*, Texas Centennial Celebration Issue, August 23, 1974.

48. Mooney, *75 Years in Victoria*, 34–40.

49. Anderson, *Handbook of Victoria County*, 6.

50. "Pages through History: 150 Years of the *Victoria Advocate*, The Petrochemical Boom: DuPont Began an Era That Forever Changed Area's Economy," *Victoria Advocate*, III, 6; *Victoria Visions* 9, no. 3 (March 1985): 1, Victoria Public Library (hereafter VPL); "Your Future in Texas at Victoria with DuPont," n.d., in VPL: Vertical File — Industry, DuPont.

51. *Victoria Visions* 9, no. 3 (March 1985): 1; "Your Future in Texas at Victoria with DuPont," VPL.

52. *South Texas Industrial Data File*, by Claude Talley, Victoria College/University of Houston Library.

53. *1979 Human Services Needs Assessment Inventory*, Golden Crescent Council of Government Records, 6.

54. Anderson, *Handbook of Victoria County*, 29.

55. Table 5, "Population of Incorporated Places of 10,000 or More from Earliest Census to 1960, U.S. Bureau of the Census," *U.S. Census of Population: 1960, General Social and Economic Characteristics, Texas, Final Report PC (1)-45C* (U.S. Government Printing Office, Washington, D.C., 1962).

56. *Victoria: Comprehensive Plan*, I-21, Golden Crescent Council of Government Records.

57. Letter from Vaughn M. Bryant to W. R. McCright (Chairman of the Victoria Human Relations Council), dated December 23, 1952; signed affidavit dated September 22, 1952, by Fausto Ramírez to Minnie Molina, Notary Public, Victoria County, both at Texas State Archives, GNC Discrimination Files, Victoria County Folder.

58. Letter from Ed Idar to Vaughn Bryant, dated December 15, 1952, Texas State Archives, GNC Discrimination Files, Victoria County Folder.

59. Letter from Ed Idar to Vaughn Bryant, dated May 8, 1952, Texas State Archives, GNC Discrimination Files, Victoria County Folder.

60. Letter from W. R. McCright to Vaughn Bryant, dated May 29, 1952; letter from

Ed Idar to Vaughn Bryant, dated June 3, 1952, Texas State Archives, GNC Discrimination Files, Victoria County Folder. In his letter McCright noted that the committee had met with "two Latin-Americans" and written a correction that was later published in the *Victoria Advocate*. The letter ended with the sentence, "Everyone is happy."

61. "Blacklisted Counties—Mexican Government 1952—? (illegible)," Texas State Archives, GNC Discrimination Files, Folder 16.

62. Unsigned, undated, unaddressed memo in Texas State Archives, GNC Discrimination Files, Victoria County Folder.

Chapter 2

1. Grimes, *300 Years in Victoria County*, 557; St. Mary's Parish and Our Lady of Lourdes Parish, Catholic Archives of Texas, San Antonio (hereafter CASA).

2. Our Lady of Lourdes Parish, CASA.

3. Lawrence Mosqueda, in *Chicanos, Catholicism, and Political Ideology*, argues that the relationship between Mexican Americans and the Catholic Church has been dynamic. He further posits that religion has served a dual social purpose, at once masking reality and protesting it. Moreover, "Religion, or more specifically the Catholic Church, can be seen as a form of social control not because it forcibly stops actions, but because it limits action and options," 17.

4. 1910 Annual Parish Report, Folder "1860–1933," St. Mary's Parish (SMP), CASA.

5. Jay P. Dolan and Gilberto M. Hinojosa, *Mexican Americans and the Catholic Church, 1900–1965*, 52.

6. Resume: (Mexican Church at Victoria), Folder "1913–1949," Our Lady of Sorrows (hereafter OLS) files CASA; *Golden Jubilee*, 20, OLS Parish files—Victoria, State Catholic Archives (hereafter SCA).

7. Resume: (Mexican Church at Victoria), Folder "1913–1949," OLS files, CASA.

8. Letter from Father F. X. Heck to Rev. J. W. Shaw, D.D., San Antonio, Texas, dated November 17, 1913, Folder "1913–1949," OLS files, CASA.

9. Resume: (Mexican Church at Victoria), Folder "1913–1949," OLS files, CASA; *Golden Jubilee*, 20, OLS Parish files, SCA.

10. 1910 Annual Parish Report, Folder "1860–1933," SMP files, CASA.

11. Unsigned, undated memo in Incarnate Word and Blessed Sacrament, Record Books, Incarnate Word of the Blessed Sacrament (IWBS) Archives, Victoria, Texas. Copy in possession of the author.

12. *Golden Jubilee*, 17–18, and "Our Lady of Sorrows Parish," undated document in OLS files, SCA.

13. Letter from Mother M. Gerard, Superiorese General in Victoria, to Rev.

James C. Brunner, Superintendent of Catholic Schools, San Antonio, Texas, Folder "through 1979," OLS files, CASA.

14. Letter from Heck to Shaw, dated February 2, 1914, Folder "1860–1933," SMP files, CASA.

15. Letter from Fr. F. X. Heck to Rev. J. W. Shaw, dated January 9, 1917, Folder "1913–1949," OLS files, CASA.

16. Letter from Rev. J. W. Shaw to Fr. F. X. Heck, dated January 10,1917, Folder "1913–1949," OLS files, CASA.

17. Letter from Lucey to Fr. Daniel E. Giorgi, dated June 5, 1943, Folder "1913–1949," OLS files, CASA.

18. Document entitled "Victoria-Our Lady of Sorrows," dated July, 1943, Folder "1913–1949," OLS files, CASA.

19. Letter from Giorgi to Rev. James T. Lockwood, dated August 3, 1944, Folder "1913–1949," OLS files, CASA.

20. Letter from Fr. Beck to J. T. Lockwood in San Antonio, dated September 20, 1944, Folder "1913–1949," OLS files, CASA.

21. Memo from Lucey to Lockwood, dated September 22, 1944, Folder "1913–1949," OLS files, CASA.

22. Letter from Lockwood to Giorgi, dated December 6, 1944, and reply, from Giorgi to Lucey, dated December 12, 1944, both in Folder "1913–1949," OLS files, CASA.

23. *Golden Jubilee*, 25, OLS; Isabel Durón, interview with the author, July 11, 1997.

24. Jeanette Rodríguez, *Our Lady of Guadalupe: Faith and Empowerment among Mexican-American Women.*

25. Durón interview.

26. *Golden Jubilee*, 25, OLS; Durón interview; Guadalupe Alemán, interview with the author, July 14, 1997.

27. Durón interview.

28. Durón interview. Durón was a founding member of the Guadalupanas.

29. Isidore Ozuna, interview with the author, June 12, 1996; "Isidore N. Ozuna: Retirement Ceremony, Naval Reserve Center Naval Air Station Corpus Christi, Texas, May 1, 1985," in Isidore Ozuna Papers and copy in possession of the author.

30. *Golden Jubilee*, 34, OLS; Recruitment memo, Catholic War Veterans, Department of Texas, Isidore Ozuna Papers, copy in possession of the author; Ozuna interview.

31. *Golden Jubilee*, 34, OLS; Recruitment memo, Catholic War Veterans, Department of Texas, in Isidore Ozuna Papers and copy in possession of the author.

32. *Golden Jubilee*, 35, OLS; *Victoria Advocate*, March 28, 1965.

33. *Golden Jubilee*, 36, OLS.

34. Ozuna interview.

35. *Golden Jubilee*, 2, OLS.

36. Janie Martínez, "Our Lady of Sorrows Ballet Folklorico—A Flower That Keeps on Blooming," 1.

37. Janie Martínez, interview with the author, July 17, 1997.

38. Martínez interview.

39. *Victoria Advocate*, October 23, 1963; October 16, 1966; August 8, 1968; March 10, 1970.

40. Martínez interview.

41. Richelle Martínez Pulido, interview with the author, July 18, 1997.

42. Pulido interview. It is important to note, however, that the CYO of the 1960s also engaged in prayer and stressed mass attendance. But in that era CYO sought to achieve personal spirituality, whereas in the 1980s it pursued the development of a greater sense of social responsibility.

43. Pulido interview.

44. *Golden Jubilee*, 42–44, OLS.

45. Dolan and Hinojosa, *Mexican Americans and the Catholic Church*, 116.

46. Frank Ortiz, interview with the author, November 15, 1996.

47. OLS, *Golden Jubilee*, 42–44. In fact, the *Golden Jubilee* adds that so powerful is the process of faith development that it is controversial and some Catholics perceive it to be a form of brainwashing.

48. Dolan and Hinojosa, *Mexican Americans and the Catholic Church*, 117.

49. Ibid., 118.

50. It must be noted that some Cursillistas did indeed leave the Catholic Church for various Protestant sects that focused on the importance of the individual. As Lawrence Mosqueda points out, the act of leaving the Church was one of conscious choice. Movement away from the Church was not the result of changes within the Church itself, but rather, of changes within individuals "who created and/or were caught in a shifting consciousness based on objective conditions that no longer could be rationally justified." Mosqueda, *Chicano, Catholicism, and Political Ideology*, 108. While Mosqueda makes such arguments in light of shifting political consciousness, generally, in Victoria such movements appear to have been the result of shifting religious consciousness instead.

51. Dolan and Hinojosa, *Mexican Americans and the Catholic Church*, 123.

52. This incident was highly controversial and acted to divide not only parishioners but also families. The evidence relating to this incident is based on several confidential interviews with various participants.

53. Letter from Soila Rincón to Archbishop Francis Furey, dated November 8, 1971, Folder "through 1979," OLS files, CASA.

54. Letter from parishioners to Reverend Harding in Baltimore, Maryland, dated November 13, 1971, Folder "through 1979," OLS files, CASA. There were several signers with the same last names on the letter. The most common names were Prybil, Edwards, Pozzi, Holzheizer, O'Connor, and Thomas.

55. Letter from Robert Álvarez to Reverend Patrick Flores Auxiliary Bishop of San Antonio, dated November 9, 1971, Folder "through 1979," OLS files, CASA.

56. Letter to Álvarez from Flores, dated November 5, 1971, Folder "through 1979," OLS files, CASA.

57. "Walking Humbly in Victoria," 4.

58. Dolan and Hinojosa, *Mexican Americans and the Catholic Church*, 111.

59. "Walking Humbly in Victoria," 5.

60. Ibid.

61. Sister Odelia Koreneck, interview with the author, July 15, 1997.

62. Sr. Koreneck interview.

63. Ibid.

64. Ibid.; "Gulf Coast Organizing Effort Delegate Assembly," program, dated December 3, 1989, Sister Odelia Koreneck Papers.

65. Roberto R. Treviño, "*La Fe*: Catholicism and Mexican Americans in Houston, 1911–1972."

Chapter 3

1. David Montejano, *Anglos and Mexicans in the Making of Texas, 1836–1986*, 160, 191; Rodolfo Acuña, *Occupied America: A History of Chicanos*, 310.

2. Guadalupe San Miguel, "*Let All of Them Take Heed*": Mexican Americans and the Campaign for Educational Equality in Texas, 1910–1981, 18–20.

3. Gilbert G. Gonzalez, *Chicano Education in the Era of Segregation*.

4. Ibid., 16–22.

5. Arnoldo De León, *Ethnicity in the Sunbelt: A History of Mexican Americans in Houston*, 24–26.

6. San Miguel, "*Let All of Them Take Heed*," 11–13, 32–58.

7. Annie Webb Blanton and R. L. Ragsdale, *Texas High Schools: History and the Social Sciences*, Bulletin 124, October 15, 1920, Austin, Department of Education of the State of Texas, 8.

8. Carlos E. Cortés, "Mexicans," 713, in Stephan Thernstrom, ed., *Harvard Encyclopedia of American Ethnic Groups*; San Miguel, "*Let All of Them Take Heed*," 46.

9. Arnoldo De León, "A People with Many Histories: Mexican Americans in Texas," 154, in Ben Procter and Archie McDonald eds., *The Texas Heritage*.

10. San Miguel, *"Let All of Them Take Heed,"* 64–67.

11. Richard A. García, *Rise of the Mexican American Middle Class: San Antonio, 1929–1941*, 183.

12. Abel Delgado, interview with the author, January 23, 1995.

13. Henry Wolff, "Henry Wolff's Journal: Carlos Delgado Was a Cut Above," *Victoria Advocate*, March 17, 1987; *Victoria Advocate*, August 8, 1993; Delgado interview.

14. Delgado interview; Paul S. Taylor, *An American-Mexican Frontier: Nueces County, Texas*, 210; Acuña, *Occupied America*, 310–11.

15. Robbie Parkman, *Victoria Schools, 1824–1980*, 39.

16. Although Mexican American students are not cited specifically as the target of this rule, the timing is certainly suspicious. Further, Mexicans had traditionally been seen by whites as dirty and diseased. See De León, *They Called Them Greasers*.

17. VISD Board minutes, October 11, 1920. G. T. Bludworth and D. B. Taylor (State Supervisors of Negro Education), *Negro Education in Texas: Special Activities and Industrial Aid*, Austin, Department of Education of the State of Texas, October 1926, 3; VISD Board minutes, February 11, 1920. Additionally, this fear of contamination remained a statewide phenomenon. Over the subsequent decades state officials addressed the need to protect "American" children who had been taught the need for cleanliness at home. This issue was raised to reinforce the notion that it was doubly important and difficult to teach habits of cleanliness to "little foreign speaking children who have had no home training and few facilities to encourage them in habits of cleanliness." In the context of this pronouncement "foreign speaking" referred primarily to Mexican-descent children, but the notion of "dirtiness" was applied to African Americans as well. The introduction of a report on "Negro Education in Texas" took pride in recent achievements in the area of Negro education such as "a broader and more practical course of study, including instruction in sanitation, health and correct living standards" (George I. Sánchez and Henry Otto, eds., *A Guide for Teachers of Spanish-Speaking Children in the Primary Grades*, Bulletin 464, Austin, Department of Education of the State of Texas, 1946, 17).

18. San Miguel, *"Let All of Them Take Heed,"* 67–86.

19. Mario T. García, *Mexican Americans*, 55–59; San Miguel, *"Let All of Them Take Heed,"* 242, 118–19, 123–28, 133–34; Acuña, *Occupied America*, 330; Gonzalez, *Chicano Education*, 136–37, 158.

20. VISD Board minutes, August 17, 1955.

21. VISD Board minutes, March 5, 1954 and August 17, 1955.

22. VISD Board minutes, August 17, 1955.

23. VISD Board minutes, April 16, 1956.

24. VISD Board minutes, February 3, 1958.

25. Manuel Velasco, interview with the author, July 2, 1997. Velasco served one term from 1958–60.

26. John Artero, interview with the author, May, 5, 1995; "Yarbrough Ousted by Mrs. Campbell," *Victoria Advocate*, April 5, 1964, 1A.

27. VISD Board minutes, August 19, 1971.

28. "Trustees Hear Protest on 'One Way' Bus Plan," *Victoria Advocate*, September 17, 1971, 1A.

29. "VISD Threatened with State Action," *Victoria Advocate*, October 31, 1975, 1A.

30. C. R. Callis, letter to the editor, *Victoria Advocate*, December 23, 1975.

31. Beatrice Flores, letter to the editor, *Victoria Advocate*, September 7, 1976.

32. VISD Board minutes, March 2, 1971.

33. VISD Board minutes, April 19, 1973.

34. VISD Board minutes, August 16, 1973.

35. "School Board Discusses Minority Hiring Practices," *Victoria Advocate*, October 18, 1974, 1A.

36. "Hearing Completed in School Dispute," *Victoria Advocate*, September 9, 1976, 1A.

37. "Class Action OK'd in School Dispute," *Victoria Advocate*, April 20, 1977, 1A.

38. "VISD Goes on Trial," *Victoria Advocate*, August 16, 1977, 1A; Judge Owen D. Cox's Court Order in the District Court of the United States for the Southern District of Texas, Victoria Division, July 24, 1978, 3, 6, located in the Rubén Bonilla Papers, Box 11, Folder 13, Nettie Lee Benson Latin American Collection, University of Texas–Austin.

39. "Program Praised," *Victoria Advocate*, August 19, 1977, 1A.

40. Judge Owen D. Cox's Order in the García case, in the District Court of the United States for the Southern District of Texas, Victoria Division, July 24, 1978, 13–15.

41. Court Order in the District Court of the United States for the Southern District of Texas, Victoria Division, July 24, 1978, 9.

42. *Victoria Advocate*, July 25, 1978.

43. Ibid.

44. "Memorial Scholarship Set," *Victoria Advocate*, September 15, 1982, 6A.

45. *U.S.A. v. VISD*, filed in Federal District Court, Southern District of Texas, Victoria, Texas, case V-86-17; *Victoria Advocate*, June 4, 1986, July 23, 1986, and August 26, 1986.

46. *Victoria Advocate*, March 19, 1987 and March 20, 1987.

47. "Judges Alter Language," *Victoria Advocate*, April 3, 1987, 1A.

48. Letter to the editor, *Victoria Advocate*, March 31, 1987.

49. Chris Rivera, letter to the editor, *Victoria Advocate*, April 2, 1987; Aquilla Adams, letter to the editor, *Victoria Advocate*, April 2, 1987.

50. "Federal Judges Due Look at Access Policy," *Victoria Advocate*, June 4, 1987, 1A.

51. "Voters Ask for Agenda Ruling," *Victoria Advocate*, April 29, 1987, 1A.

52. "VISD's Policy Questioned," *Victoria Advocate*, July 8, 1987, 1A.

53. Sworn affidavit in District Court case CA. V-87-16, District Court, Victoria, Texas.

54. San Miguel, *"Let All of Them Take Heed,"* 18–19.

55. *Snapshot, 1991–92 School District Profiles*, Division of Policy Planning and Education (Austin: Texas Education Agency, 1993), 249.

56. Angela Valenzuela, in *Subtractive Schooling: U.S.-Mexican Youth and the Politics of Caring*, demonstrates the ways in which an assimilationist curriculum combined with negative teacher attitudes continues to mar Mexican American educational potential.

Chapter 4

1. This chapter's title is the motto of the American Citizens' Social Club.

2. Matt López, interview with the author, February 9, 1995; Josie González, interview with the author, February 23, 1995.

3. American Citizens' Social Club Constitution, 3; López interview.

4. Constitution of the American Citizens' Social Club; López interview; Solís interview.

5. López interview; Solís interview; Constitution of the American Citizens' Social Club.

6. Constitution of the American Citizens' Social Club, 3; López interview.

7. *Victoria Advocate*, August 7, 1960.

8. *Victoria Advocate*, February 9, 1964 and March 28, 1965; Constitution of the American Citizens' Social Club, 2.

9. *Victoria Advocate*, October 11, 1960.

10. Judge Frank Crain, interview with the author, May 7, 1996; Solís interview; letter from Ralph Castillo to Hector P. García, no date, Folder 47.23, Hector P. García (hereafter HPG) Papers, Texas A&M University–Corpus Christi.

11. López interview; *Victoria Advocate*, January 5, 1962.

12. *Victoria Advocate*, January 5, 1962, January 11, 1962, and January 12, 1962. Charging a poll tax receipt for a dance was a practice also carried on by the American G.I.

Forum. Letter from Jessie Carrizales, president of the American G.I. Forum in Seguin, Texas, to Hector P. García, dated January 13, 1951, Folder 147.11, HPG Papers.

13. *Victoria Advocate*, September 21, 1968 and August 28, 1969; undated letter from Ralph Castillo to John Young on behalf of ACSC, Folder 47.23, HPG Papers.

14. López interview; Solís interview.

15. González interview.

16. Ibid.

17. López interview.

18. District Court case 19,904, in District Clerk's Office, County of Victoria, Victoria, Texas.

19. Minutes of American Citizens' Social Club meeting, December, 1969, as found in District Clerk's office, case 19,904.

20. Plaintiff's Original Petition, *American Citizens' Social Club v. Matt López et al.*, filed in District Court of Victoria County on October 10, 1971, docket 19,904; minutes of ACSC meeting on December 9, 1969, found in judgment records for case 19,904, Victoria District Court, District Clerk's Office; Interrogatories Propounded to Defendants, dated January 21, 1972, Defendants' Answers to Plaintiffs' Interrogatories (no date).

21. Minutes of American Citizens' Social Club meeting of December 9, 1970, as found in District Clerk's files for case 19,904.

22. Plaintiff's Original Petition, *American Citizens' Social Club v. Matt López et al.*, filed in District Court of Victoria County, October 7, 1971, case 19,904.

23. Plaintiff's Second Amended Original Petition, filed January 7, 1972, case 19,904.

24. Letter from Jesse Gámez (attorney for the ACSCI) to Judge Frank Crain, dated March 8, 1973.

25. "Settlement Made in Suit by Club," *Victoria Advocate*, June 20, 1973.

26. *Victoria Advocate*, January 18, 1979.

27. Ibid., June 24, 1956.

28. Ibid., September 4, 1955.

29. Ibid., May 19, 1956.

30. "The American G. I. Forum First Annual Convention Program," 1949; letter from Hector P. García to Mr. Gerald Saldaña, dated March 13, 1954, both in HPG Papers, Folder 141.13.

31. Letter from Ed Idar to the editor of *The Union Newspaper*, dated February 2, 1954, Folder 142.13, HPG Papers.

32. Folder 147.12, HPG Papers.

33. *Victoria Advocate*, October 18, 1957; October 27, 1957; March 5, 1958.

34. Félix Monclova, interview with the author, May 15, 1996.

35. *Victoria Advocate*, May 1, 1970.

36. Luis Chacón, interview with the author, June 11, 1997.

37. "NLRB Decision and Order," *Victoria Advocate*, June 20, 1973.

38. Chacón interview.

39. "NLRB Decision and Order."

40. Ibid.; *Victoria Advocate*, May 28, 1972.

41. *Victoria Advocate*, May 28, 1972.

42. Ibid.

43. Ibid.; *Victoria Advocate*, November 2, 1973 and November 3, 1973.

44. Press release, dated November 1, 1973, *Victoria Advocate*, Clippings File, "Farah" Folder.

45. This phrase is adopted from Gary Gerstle's *Working-Class Americanism: The Politics of Labor in a Textile City, 1914–1960*.

46. Chacón interview.

47. Letter to Lucinda Cornish, administrator of Care Inn South, from LULAC Council 626, dated September 29, 1977, in Lucille Martínez García Papers; "LULAC Charges Nursing Home," *Victoria Advocate*, September 30, 1977, as reprinted in the *LULAC Word* newsletter, 1, no. 5, October, 1977, 3, in Lucille Martínez García Papers.

48. *LULAC Word* newsletter 1, no. 5, October, 1977, 3.

49. *Victoria Advocate*, October 5, 1977.

50. Ibid., October 25, 1977.

51. Letter from Rocky Martínez to Rubén Bonilla, dated June 14, 1978, Rubén Bonilla Office Files, Texas State Director Papers, 1978–1978, Box 4, Folder 11, in the Benson Latin American Collection, University of Texas–Austin.

52. *LULAC: 50 Years of Serving Hispanics*, in Lucille Martínez García Papers.

53. Lupe Hernández and Lupita Hernández, interviews with the author, January 25, 1996.

54. Hernández interviews.

55. Hernández interviews; also see the *Victoria Advocate*, September 15, 1983. García's experiences are recounted in chapter 4 of this work. Council 4319 had held a scholarship awards banquet since 1981 but changed the name to honor García in 1984.

56. *Victoria Advocate*, September 14, 1988.

57. Benjamin Márquez, *LULAC: The Evolution of a Mexican American Political Organization*, 93; Hernández interviews; González interview.

58. "Fifth Annual Cris García Memorial Scholarship Banquet Program," 1986, Lupe and Lupita Hernández Papers; Hernández interviews.

59. "Sixth Annual Memorial Scholarship and Awards Banquet," 1987 program; "Fifth Annual Cris García Memorial Scholarship Banquet Program," 1986, both from Lupe and Lupita Hernández Papers.

60. Letter from Lucille Martínez García to Rubén Bonilla, dated April 11, 1979, Rubén Bonilla Office Files, Texas State Director Papers, 1978–1979, Box 4, Folder 11, Benson Latin American Collection, University of Texas–Austin.

61. Márquez, *LULAC*, 89.

62. Hernández interviews.

63. *Victoria Advocate*, June 6, 1967.

64. Ibid., December 2, 1967.

65. *Victoria Advocate*, June 20, 1969 and November 25, 1978; *Victoria Advocate*, photo with caption, November 23, 1980. For a discussion of the role of conjunto music as an element of class distinctions see Manuel H. Peña, *The Texas-Mexican Conjunto: History of Working-Class Music*.

66. *Victoria Advocate*, March 21, 1989 and April 15, 1990.

67. Ibid., July 2, 1970, February 21, 1974, September 8, 1974, and March 27, 1975.

68. Ibid., November 24, 1982.

Chapter 5

1. For more on South Texas political machines see Evan Anders, *Boss Rule in South Texas: The Progressive Era*. Anders discusses machine politics within the context of rural Texas during the Progressive Era. Another work that addresses this period in Texas history and sheds light on the political psyche that caused Progressivism to express itself differently in Texas than in other parts of the country is Norman D. Brown's *Hood, Bonnet, and Little Brown Jug: South Texas Politics, 1921–1928*. For a newer interpretation of the role of South Texas political machines, see Gilberto Quezada's *Border Boss: Manuel B. Bravo and Zapata County*.

2. Navarro, *Cristal Experiment*, 25–26; Ralph Guzman, "The Function of Anglo-American Racism in the Political Development of *Chicanos*," 20, in *La Causa Política: A Chicano Politics Reader*, ed. F. Chris Garcia; López interview.

3. Hildo Luera, interview with the author, July 10, 1997.

4. López interview; Charlie Kidder, interview with the author, July 24, 1996; Velasco interview.

5. George Santiago, interview with the author May 23, 1993; López interview; Solís interview.

6. Richard Anthony Santillán, "Latino Political Development in the Southwest and the Midwest Regions: A Comparative Overview, 1915–1989," 118, in *Latinos and Political Coalitions: Political Empowerment for the 1990s*, ed. Roberto E. Villareal, Norma G. Hernandez, and Howard D. Neighbor.

7. Velasco interview; VISD Board minutes, 1957–1959, 247.

8. For a deeper examination of the kinds of pressure on Mexican American politi-

cal candidates, see Mario T. García's "The Politics of Status: The Election of Raymond L. Telles as Mayor of El Paso, 1957," in *Mexican Americans,* and *The Making of a Mexican American Mayor: Raymond L. Telles of El Paso.*

9. Benjamin Márquez, *Power and Politics in a Chicano Barrio: A Study of Mobilization Efforts and Community Power in El Paso,* 32. Márquez notes how Raymond Telles, in running for and winning the mayoralty of El Paso in 1957, had to prove to the Anglo voters his commitment to "all the people" despite the fact that he was "a prime example of acculturation: a lieutenant colonel in the United States Air Force, a Korean War veteran, and a small businessman with a conservative political philosophy." For more on the election of Raymond Telles, see also Mario T. García, *Making of a Mexican American Mayor.*

10. Velasco interview.

11. *Victoria Advocate,* June 6, 1961; Velasco interview.

12. Velasco interview; Ignacio García, *United We Win: The Rise and Fall of La Raza Unida Party,* 198–205.

13. Juan Gómez-Quiñones, *Chicano Politics: Reality and Promise, 1940–1990,* 66–67; Ignacio García, *United We Win,* 9, and *Viva Kennedy,* 127–30.

14. Artero interview, June 7, 1993.

15. Armando Gutiérrez and Herbert Hirsch, "The Militant Challenge to the American Ethos: 'Chicanos,' and 'Mexican Americans,'" 88, in *La Causa Política,* ed. F. Chris Garcia. For a deeper analysis of how Anglos in one small community maintained cultural hegemony and appropriated such values as their own see Navarro, *Cristal Experiment.*

16. In December, 1966, Mexican American students walked out of Crystal City schools and registered Mexican American voters to participate in the coming spring school board elections (Rodolfo O. de la Garza et al., eds., *Chicanos and Native Americans: The Territorial Minorities,* 117); Arturo Rodríguez, interview with the author February 21, 1997.

17. Corpus Christi *Caller Times,* September 17, 1970; Arturo Rodríguez, interview with the author February 21, 1997.

18. Rodríguez interview; Luera interview.

19. *Victoria Advocate,* September 17, 1970; Corpus Christi *Caller Times,* September 17, 1970.

20. De la Garza, *Chicanos and Native Americans,* 116.

21. Rodríguez interview.

22. *Victoria Advocate,* August 19, 1972.

23. Ibid., October 30, 1974.

24. Ibid., June 30, 1974.

25. Mark R. Levy and Michael S. Kramer, "Patterns of Chicano Voting Behavior," 247–49, in *La Causa Política*, ed. F. Chris Garcia.

26. *Victoria Advocate*, November 9, 1972.

27. *Victoria Advocate*, November 6, 1974.

28. Ignacio García, *United We Win*, 197–204.

29. Márquez, *Power and Politics*, 30–31.

30. *Victoria Advocate*, March 5, 1971.

31. Luera was the son-in-law of John Artero, and was a partner in the funeral home.

32. Luera interview.

33. Ibid.

34. Victoria City Council Minutes, Minute Book 21 (October 6, 1975–October 7, 1979), May 22, 1978, Office of the City Secretary.

35. Ibid.; *Victoria Advocate*, June 9, 1978.

36. Victoria City Council Minutes, Minute Book 21, meeting of May 22, 1978, 401.

37. *Victoria Advocate*, June 11, 1978.

38. Ibid.

39. Ibid. and June 13, 1978; Victoria City Council Minutes, Minute Book 21, June 8, 1978, Office of the City Secretary.

40. *Victoria Advocate*, June 13, 1978.

41. Ibid.

42. *Victoria Advocate*, February 15, 1980.

43. Ibid.

44. Ibid.

45. Undated recommendation by the Mexican American Chamber of Commerce to the City's Charter Revision Committee. Office of the City Secretary.

46. Letter from C. C. Carsner to the Charter Revision Committee, Office of the City Secretary, dated June 17, 1980.

47. *Victoria Advocate*, April 23, 1980.

48. Ibid., July 2, 1980.

49. Ibid.

50. Ibid.; *Victoria Advocate*, October 5, 1980.

51. City Council Minutes, vol. 24, June 6, 1988, 149.

52. *Victoria Advocate*, November 5, 1980.

53. Ibid.

54. Ibid.; Knute Dietz, interview with the author, July 1, 1997; Gutiérrez interview; Crain interview.

55. *Victoria Advocate*, November 29, 1987 and December 17, 1987.

56. Ibid., April 13, 1988. Hinojosa won the absentee vote by margin of 102 to 46 in

addition to winning at Hopkins School 200 to 83, Patti Welder Middle School 125 to 103, and O'Connor Elementary School 174 to 144. Targac won in Placedo 133 to 99, Bloomington 295 to 162, and Guadalupe 198 to 57.

57. *Victoria Advocate*, October 31, 1979, January 16, 1980, January 31, 1980, and February 14, 1980. MALDEF and the SWVREP were also suing neighboring Refugio County as well as Atascosa, Medina, Uvalde, Cochran, Edwards, Lynn, Dawson, Crosby, and Castro counties for the same reason.

58. *Victoria Advocate*, February 14, 1980 and May 8, 1980.

59. Ibid., March 6, 1982.

60. Commissioners' Court Minutes, County Clerk's Office, September 21, 1984, Book 74, page 445, item 13.

61. *Victoria Advocate*, December 14, 1985.

62. Ibid., January 6, 1986.

63. Ibid., January 5, 1986.

64. Ibid., November 7, 1984.

65. Ibid.

66. *Victoria Advocate*, February 1, 1986.

67. Diana Rhodes, interview with the author, July 23, 1997; Don Truman, interview with the author, June 27, 1997.

68. Luera interview.

69. *Victoria Advocate*, August 14, 1984.

70. Ibid., November 9, 1988.

71. Ibid., March 23, 1989 and May 7, 1989.

72. López interview.

Bibliography

Libraries and Archives

Benson Latin American Collection, University of Texas–Austin.

Catholic Archives of Texas, San Antonio, (CASA). Parish Archives, Victoria, St. Mary's Parish. Parish Archives, Victoria, Our Lady of Lourdes Parish. Parish Archives, Victoria, Our Lady of Sorrows Parish.

City Council Documents, Office of the City Secretary, City of Victoria, Texas. City Council Minutes: Vol. 24, May 2, 1988; Vol. 21, May 22, 1978; Vol. 21, June 8, 1978; Vol. 24, June 6, 1988. Charter Revision Committee Files, 1980.

District Clerk Records, Victoria, County. District Court Case 19,904.

Dr. Hector P. García Papers, Texas A&M University–Corpus Christi.

Golden Crescent Council of Government Records, Victoria, Texas. "1979 Human Services Needs Assessment Inventory," Golden Crescent Council of Governments, 1979. *Victoria: Comprehensive Plan*, N.d.

Incarnate Word and Blessed Sacrament Archives, Victoria, Texas. IWBS Record Books.

Isidore Ozuna Papers, Victoria, Texas.

Lucille Martínez García Papers, Victoria, Texas.

Lupe and Lupita Hernández Papers, Victoria, Texas.

Odelia Koreneck Papers, San Antonio, Texas.

Rolando Ríos Papers, San Antonio, Texas.

Rubén Bonilla Papers. Rubén Bonilla Office Files, Texas State Director Papers, Benson Latin American Collection, University of Texas–Austin.

State Catholic Archives (CSA), Austin, Texas. Parishes file—Victoria.

Texas Education Agency Library. Austin, Texas. A Handbook of Information as to Education in Texas, 1918–1922, Bulletin 157, Department of Education of the State of Texas, 1923. Blanton, Annie Webb, R. L. Ragsdale, and Texas High Schools: History and the Social Sciences, Bulletin 124, Department of Education of the State of Texas, October, 1920. Historical and Statistical Data as to Education in Texas, January 1, 1919–January 1, 1921, Bulletin 133, Department of Education of the State of Texas, August, 1921. Bludworth, G. T., D. B. Taylor, Negro Education in Texas: Special Activities and Industrial Aid, October, 1926. Doughty, W. F., Twenty-First Biennial Report: State Superintendent of Public Instruction, State of Texas, September 1, 1916 to August 31, 1918. Austin: State Board of Education, 1918. Henderson, Katherine Bradford: Untitled Bulletin 279, Department of Education of the State of Texas, February, 1931. Martin, A. B., Gordon Worley: Social Studies in the Secondary Schools, Bulletin 503, Department of Education of the State of Texas, 1947. Sánchez, George I., Henry J. Otto: A Guide for Teachers of Spanish Speaking Children in the Primary Grades, Bulletin 464, Department of Education, State of Texas, 1946. Snapshot, 1991–91, School District Profiles, Texas Education Agency, 1993. Tanner, Myrtle, Los Caminos de Amistad: Curriculum Enrichment Materials for High Schools, Publication of Department of Education of the State of Texas, 1946.

Texas State Archives, Austin, Texas. Good Neighbor Commission Discrimination Files. *Sixty Years of Germany in America*. Victoria, Tex.: Victoria Council of Defense, N.d.

U.S. Bureau of the Census, 1920, manuscript census in Victoria Public Library.

U.S. Federal District Court Records. Court Order in Case V-86-17. Court Order in Case V-87-16. Court Order in Case V-92-006. *Rojas v. City of Victoria, et al.*

University of Texas, Perry Castañeda Library. United States Census, Area and Population of Counties, Urban and Rural: 1960 and 1950. U.S. Congress, Report of the Immigration Commission, 61st Cong., 3rd sess. (1910–1911).

Victoria Chamber of Commerce. "Employment Records." "Victoria Economics," in *Victoria Chamber of Commerce Newsletter*, Victoria, Tex., 7, no. 4, June, 1984. *Victoria: The Time and Place*, 1990.

Victoria City Directory 1900–1901. Springfield, Mo.: Interstate Directory Company, 1901.

Victoria City Directory. Springfield, Mo.: Interstate Directory Company, 1933, 1941, 1950, 1960, 1970, 1980.

Victoria College/University of Houston Library, Victoria, Texas Special Collections. Talley, Claude, *South Texas Industrial Data File*.

Victoria County Extension Service. "Victoria County Statistics," N.d.

Victoria Independent School District Board Minutes. Victoria, Texas (VISD Board). April, 1918 (exact date illegible). February 11, October 11, 1920. March 2, 1941. March 5, 1954. August 17, 1955. April 16, 1956. February 3, 1958. April, 1958 (exact date illegible). August 19, 1971. March 19, 1973. June 20, 1973. August 16, 1973. January 18, 1979.

Victoria Public Library Vertical File. *Victoria Visions* 9, no. 3, Victoria Chamber of Commerce, March, 1985. *Victoria Visions* 9, no. 8, Victoria Chamber of Commerce, October, 1985. "Your Future in Texas at Victoria with DuPont," N.d. "Victoria Comprehensive Plan." Golden Crescent Council of Governments. NLRB Decision and Order, 20 June 20, 1973. "County Population Changes, 1850–1870." "City Population Changes, 1850–1970." "Victoria Population."

Interviews

All interviews were with the author in Victoria, Texas, unless otherwise noted.

Alemán, Guadalupe. July 14, 1997.

Artero, John. June 6, 1993; May 5, 1995.

Chacón, Luis. June 11, 1997.

Crain, Frank. May 7, 1996.

Delgado, Abel. January 23, 1995.

Dietz, Knute. July 1, 1997.

Durón, Isabel. July 11, 1997.

González, Josie. February 23, 1995.

Gutiérrez, Teresa. June 15, 1993.

Hernández, Lupe. January 25, 1996.

Hernández, Lupita. January 25, 1996

Kidder, Charlie. July 24, 1996.

Koreneck, Odelia. San Antonio, Texas, July 15, 1997.

López, Matt. February 9,1995.

Luera, Hildo. July 10, 1997.

Martínez, Janie. July 17, 1997.

Monclova, Félix. May 15, 1996.

Ortiz, Frank. January 16, 1996.

Ozuna, Isidore. June 12, 1996.

Pulido, Richelle Martinez. July 18, 1997.

Rhodes, Diana. Victoria, Texas, July 23, 1996.

Rodríguez, Arturo. February 21, 1997.

Santiago, George. 4 June 4, 1993.

Solís, Carlos. May 1, 1996.

Truman, Donald. June 27, 1997.

Velasco, Manuel. Houston, Texas, July 2, 1997.

Books and Articles

Achor, Shirley. *Mexican Americans in a Dallas Barrio.* Tucson: University of Arizona Press, 1978.

Acuña, Rodolfo. *Occupied America: A History of Chicanos.* 4th ed. New York: Addison-Wesley, 1999.

Allsup, Vernon Carl. *The American G.I. Forum: Origins and Evolution.* Austin: Center for Mexican American Studies, 1982.

Alonzo, Armando, C. *Tejano Legacy: Rancheros and Settlers in South Texas, 1734–1900.* Albuquerque: University of New Mexico Press, 1998.

Anders, Evan. *Boss Rule in South Texas: The Progressive Era.* Austin: University of Texas Press, 1982.

Anderson, Penny, et al., eds. *The Handbook of Victoria County.* Austin: Texas State Historical Association, 1990.

Barker, Eugene C. *The Life of Stephen F. Austin: Founder of Texas, 1793–1836.* Nashville: Cokesbury Press, 1925.

Bauman, Richard, and Roger D. Abrahams, eds. *"And Other Neighborly Names": Social Process and Cultural Image in Texas Folklore.* Austin: University of Texas Press, 1981.

Brack, Gene. *Mexico Views Manifest Destiny, 1821–1846: An Essay on the Origins of the Mexican War.* Albuquerque: University of New Mexico Press, 1975.

Brown, Norman D. *Hood, Bonnet, and Little Brown Jug: Texas Politics, 1921–1928.* College Station: Texas A&M University Press, 1984.

Calvert, Robert A., and Arnoldo De León. *The History of Texas.* 3rd ed. Wheeling, Ill.: Harlan Davidson Press, 2002.

Calvert, Robert A., Renato Rosaldo, and Gustav L. Seligmann Jr., eds. *Chicano: The Evolution of a People.* San Francisco: Rinehart Press, 1973.

Camarillo, Albert. *Chicanos in a Changing Society: From Mexican Pueblos to American Barrios in Santa Barbara and Southern California, 1848–1930.* Cambridge: Harvard University Press, 1979.

Campbell, Randolph B. *An Empire for Slavery: The Peculiar Institution in Texas, 1821–1865.* Baton Rouge: Louisiana State University Press, 1989.

Cardoso, Lawrence. *Mexican Emigration to the United States, 1897–1930: Socio-Economic Patterns.* Tucson: University of Arizona Press, 1980.

Carroll, Peter N. *It Seemed Like Nothing Happened: America in the 1970s.* New Brunswick: Rutgers University Press, 1990.

Castañeda, Carlos Eduardo. *Our Catholic Heritage in Texas, 1519–1936.* 7 vols. Austin: Von Boeckmann-Jones, 1958.

Chávez, John R. *The Lost Land: The Chicano Image of the Southwest.* Albuquerque: University of New Mexico Press, 1984.

Christian, Carole. "Joining the American Mainstream: Texas's Mexican Americans during World War I." *Southwestern Historical Quarterly* 92 (April, 1989): 559–96.

Cohen, Lizabeth. *Making a New Deal: Industrial Workers in Chicago, 1919–1939.* New York: Cambridge University Press, 1990.

Corwin, Arthur F., and Lawrence Cardoso. "Vamos al Norte: Causes of Mass Mexican Migration," 38–66. In *Immigrants — and Immigrants: Perspectives on Mexican La-*

bor Migration to the United States, ed. Arthur F. Corwin. Westport, Conn.: Greenwood Press, 1978.

Crimm, Ana Carolina Castillo. "Success in Adversity: The Mexican Americans of Victoria County, Texas, 1800–1880." Ph.D. diss., University of Texas, Austin, 1994.

Davidson, Chandler. *Race and Class in Texas Politics.* Princeton: Princeton University Press, 1990.

De Anda, Roberto M., ed. *Chicanas and Chicanos in Contemporary Society.* Boston: Pearson Allyn and Bacon, 1995.

De la Garza, Rodolfo O., Anthony Kruszewski, and Tomás A. Arciniega. *Chicanos and Native Americans: The Territorial Minorities.* Englewood Cliffs, N.J.: Prentice-Hall, 1973.

De León, Arnoldo. *Ethnicity in the Sunbelt: A History of Mexican Americans in Houston.* College Station: Texas A&M University Press, 2001.

———. *San Angeleños: Mexican Americans in San Angelo, Texas.* San Angelo: Fort Concho Museum Press, 1985.

———. *The Tejano Community, 1836–1900.* Albuquerque: University of New Mexico Press, 1982.

———. *They Called Them Greasers: Anglo Attitudes toward Mexicans in Texas, 1821–1900.* Austin: University of Texas Press, 1983.

Dobie, J. Frank. *The Longhorns.* Boston: Little, Brown and Co., 1941.

———. *A Vaquero of the Brush Country.* Dallas: Southwest Press, 1929.

Dolan, Jay P. *The American Catholic Experience: A History from Colonial Times to the Present.* Notre Dame, Ind.: University of Notre Dame Press, 1992.

———. *The Immigrant Church: New York's Irish and German Catholics, 1815–1865.* Notre Dame, Ind.: University of Notre Dame Press, 1975.

Dolan, Jay P., and Gilberto M. Hinojosa. *Mexican Americans and the Catholic Church, 1900–1965.* Notre Dame, Ind.: University of Notre Dame Press, 1994.

Fehrenbach, T. R. *Lone Star: A History of Texas and the Texans.* New York: Collier, 1968.

Foley, Douglas E., et al. *From Peones to Politicos: Class and Ethnicity in a South Texas Town, 1900–1987.* Austin: University of Texas Press, 1988.

Foley, Neil. *The White Scourge: Mexicans, Blacks, and Poor Whites in Texas Cotton Culture.* Berkeley: University of California Press, 1997.

Fox, Anne A., and Thomas R. Hester. *An Archaeological Survey of Coleto Creek, Victoria and Goliad Counties, Texas.* San Antonio: Center for Archaeological Research, University of Texas, San Antonio, 1976.

Frantz, Joe B. *Texas.* New York: W. W. Norton, 1976.

Garcia, F. Chris, ed. *La Causa Política: A Chicano Politics Reader.* Notre Dame, Ind.: University of Notre Dame Press, 1974.

García, Ignacio. *United We Win: The Rise and Fall of La Raza Unida Party.* Tucson: University of Arizona Press, 1989.

———. *Viva Kennedy: Mexican Americans in Search of Camelot.* College Station: Texas A&M University Press, 2000.

García, Mario T. *Desert Immigrants: The Mexicans of El Paso, 1880–1920.* New Haven: Yale University Press, 1981.

———. *The Making of a Mexican American Mayor: Raymond L. Telles of El Paso.* El Paso: Texas Western Press, 1998.

———. *Mexican Americans: Leadership, Ideology, and Identity, 1930–1969.* New Haven: Yale University Press, 1989.

García, Richard A. *Rise of the Mexican American Middle Class: San Antonio, 1929–1941.* College Station: Texas A&M University Press, 1991.

Gerstle, Gary. *Working-Class Americanism: The Politics of Labor in a Textile City, 1914–1960.* Cambridge: Cambridge University Press, 1989.

Gómez-Quiñones, Juan. *Chicano Politics: Reality and Promise, 1940–1990.* Albuquerque: University of New Mexico Press, 1990.

———. *The Roots of Chicano Politics, 1600–1940.* Albuquerque: University of New Mexico Press, 1994.

Gonzalez, Gilbert G. *Chicano Education in the Era of Segregation.* Philadelphia: Balch Institute Press, 1990.

Grant, Madison. *The Passing of the Great Race: Or, the Racial Basis of European History.* New York: Arno Press, 1970.

Grimes, Roy. *300 Years in Victoria County.* Victoria, Tex.: Victoria Advocate Publishing Company, 1968.

Griswold del Castillo, Richard. *The Los Angeles Barrio, 1850–1890: A Social History.* Berkeley: University of California Press, 1980.

Hammett, A. B. J. *The Empresario: Don Martin de Leon.* Waco: Texian Press, 1973.

Handlin, Oscar. *The Uprooted: The Epic Story of the Great Migrations That Made the American People.* Boston: Little, Brown, 1951.

Hardin, Stephen L. *Texian Iliad: A Military History of the Texas Revolution, 1835–1836.* Austin: University of Texas Press, 1994.

Hauschild, Henry. *The Victoria Sesquicentennial Scrapbook.* Victoria, Tex.: American Bank of Commerce, 1974.

Haynes, Sam W. *Soldiers of Misfortune: The Somervell and Mier Expeditions.* Austin: University of Texas Press, 1990.

Hernández, José Amaro. *Mutual Aid for Survival: The Case of the Mexican American.* Malabar, Fla.: Krieger, 1983.

Higham, John. *Strangers in the Land: Patterns of American Nativism, 1860–1925.* New York: Atheneum, 1966.

Hurtado, Juan. "An Attitudinal Study of Social Distance between the Mexican American and the Church." Ph.D. diss., U.S. International University, 1977.

Huson, Hobart. *Refugio: A Comprehensive History of Refugio County from Aboriginal Times to 1955.* 2 Vols. Woodsboro, Tex.: Rooke Foundation, 1956.

Ignatiev, Noel. *How the Irish Became White.* New York: Routledge, 1995.

John, Elizabeth A. H. *Storms Brewed in Other Men's Worlds: The Confrontation of Indians, Spanish, and French in the Southwest, 1540–1795.* College Station: Texas A&M University Press, 1975.

Johnson, Benjamin. *Revolution in Texas.* New Haven: Yale University Press, 2003.

Kibbe, Pauline. *Latin Americans in Texas.* Albuquerque: University of New Mexico Press, 1946.

Kingrea, Nellie Ward. *History of the First Ten Years of the Texas Good Neighbor Commission.* Fort Worth: Texas Christian University Press, 1954.

Kiser, George and Martha. *Mexican Workers in the United States: Historical and Political Perspectives.* Albuquerque: University of New Mexico Press, 1979.

Labbe, Dolores Egger. *Jim Crow Comes to Church.* New York: Arno Press, 1978.

Linn, John Joseph. *Reminiscences of 50 Years in Texas.* Austin: The Steck Company, 1935.

Luconi, Stefano. *From Paesani to White Ethnics: The Italian Experience in Philadelphia.* Albany: State University of New York Press, 2001.

Lukes, Edward. *DeWitt Colony of Texas.* Austin: Jenkins Publishing Company, The Pemberton Press, 1976.

LULAC: 50 Years of Serving Hispanics, Golden Anniversary, 1929–1979. Corpus Christi: Baldwin Printing Company, 1979.

Maríl, Robert Lee. *The Poorest of Americans: The Mexican Americans of the Lower Rio Grande Valley of Texas.* Notre Dame, Ind.: University of Notre Dame Press, 1989.

Márquez, Benjamin. *LULAC: The Evolution of a Mexican American Political Organization.* Austin: University of Texas Press, 1993.

———. *Power and Politics in a Chicano Barrio: A Study of Mobilization Efforts and Community Power in El Paso.* Lanham, Md.: University Press of America, 1985.

Martínez, Janie. "Our Lady of Sorrows Ballet Folklorico—A Flower That Keeps on Blooming." *Catholic Lighthouse* 5 (Fall, 1996): 1–2.

Matovina, Timothy. *Tejano Religion and Ethnicity: San Antonio, 1821–1869.* Austin: University of Texas Press, 1995.

Meier, Matt, and Feliciano Rivera. *The Chicanos: A History of Mexican Americans.* New York: Hill and Wang, 1972.

Meyer, Michael C., and William L. Sherman. *The Course of Mexican History*. 4th ed. New York: Oxford University Press, 1991.

Mirandé, Alfredo. *The Chicano Experience: An Alternative Perspective*. Notre Dame, Ind.: University of Notre Dame Press, 1985.

Montejano, David. *Anglos and Mexicans in the Making of Texas, 1836–1986*. Austin: University of Texas Press, 1987.

Mooney, Booth. *75 Years in Victoria*. Victoria, Tex.: Victoria Bank and Trust, 1950.

Moore, Joan. *Mexican Americans*. Englewood Cliffs, N.J.: Prentice-Hall, 1970.

Mosqueda, Lawrence. *Chicanos, Catholicism, and Political Ideology*. Lanham, Md.: University Press of America, 1986.

Nance, Joseph. *After San Jacinto: The Texas-Mexican Frontier, 1836–1841*. Austin: University of Texas Press, 1963.

———. *Attack and Counterattack: The Texas-Mexican Frontier, 1842*. Austin: University of Texas Press, 1964.

Navarro, Armando. "The Evolution of Chicano Politics." *Aztlán* 5, no. 1 (Spring, 1974): 57–84.

———. *Mexican American Youth Organization: Avant-Garde of the Chicano Movement*. Austin: University of Texas Press, 1995.

———. *The Cristal Experiment: A Chicano Struggle for Community Control*. Madison: University of Wisconsin Press, 1998.

Neal, Job West. "The Policy of the United States toward Immigration from Mexico." Master's thesis, University of Texas, 1941.

Newcomb, William W. *Indians of Texas: From Prehistoric to Modern Times*. Austin: University of Texas Press, 1961.

Olmsted, Frederick Law. *A Journey through Texas: Or a Saddle Trip on the Southwestern Frontier*. Austin: University of Texas Press, 1978.

Olson, James. *Catholic Immigrants in America*. Chicago: Nelson Hall, 1987.

Ortego, Philip D. "The Education of Mexican Americans," 157–72. In *The Chicanos: Mexican American Voices*, ed. Edward Ludwig and James Santibañez. Baltimore: Penguin, 1971.

Our Lady of Sorrows Parish. *Golden Jubilee Souvenir Book*. Victoria, Tex.: Our Lady of Sorrows, 1968.

"Pages through History: 150 Years of the *Victoria Advocate*," Victoria Tex.: Victoria Advocate, 1996.

Parkman, Robbie. "Victoria Schools, 1824–1980." Victoria, Tex.: Victoria Independent School District, 1980.

Peña, Manuel. *The Texas-Mexican Conjunto: History of a Working-Class Music*. Austin: University of Texas Press, 1985.

Petty, F. W., Jr., ed. *History of Victoria County*. Victoria, TX: BookMart, 1961.

Proctor, Ben, and Archie McDonald, eds. *The Texas Heritage*. 3rd ed. Wheeling, Ill.: Harlan Davidson, 1998.

Quezada, Gilberto. *Border Boss: Manuel B. Bravo and Zapata County*. College Station: Texas A&M University Press, 1999.

Rangel, Jorge, and Carlos Alcalá. "De Jure Segregation of *Chicanos* in Texas Schools." *Harvard Civil Rights — Civil Liberties Law Review* 7 (March, 1972): 307–91.

Reisler, Mark. *By the Sweat of Their Brow: Mexican Immigrant Labor in the United States, 1900–1940*. Westport, Conn.: Greenwood Press, 1976.

Richardson, Rupert, Adrian Anderson, and Ernest Wallace. *Texas: The Lone Star State*. 7th ed. Upper Saddle River, N.J.: Prentice-Hall, 1997.

Riddell, Adalijza Sosa, and Robert Aguallo Jr. "A Case of *Chicano* Politics: Parlier, California." *Aztlán* 9 (Double Issue, 1978): 1–27.

Rodríguez, Jeanette. *Our Lady of Guadalupe: Faith and Empowerment among Mexican-American Women*. Austin: University of Texas Press, 1994.

Roediger, David. *The Wages of Whiteness: Race and the Making of the American Working Class*. New York: Verso, 1991.

Rose, Victor. *Some Historical Facts in Regard to the Settlement of Victoria, Texas, Its Progress and Present Status*. Laredo: Daily Times Print, 1883.

Rosenbaum, Robert J. *Mexicano Resistance in the Southwest: "The Sacred Right of Self-Preservation."* Austin: University of Texas Press, 1982.

San Miguel, Guadalupe, Jr. "The Struggle against Separate and Unequal Schools: Middle Class Mexican Americans and the Desegregation Campaign in Texas, 1929–1957." *History of Education Quarterly* 23 (Fall, 1983): 343–59.

———. *"Let All of Them Take Heed": Mexican Americans and the Campaign for Educational Equality in Texas, 1910–1981*. Austin: University of Texas Press, 1987.

Sánchez, George J. *Becoming Mexican American: Ethnicity, Culture and Identity in Chicano Los Angeles, 1900–1945*. New York: Oxford University Press, 1993.

Santillán, Richard Anthony. "Latino Political Development in the Southwest and the Midwest Regions: A Comparative Overview, 1915–1989," 99–113. In *Latinos and Political Coalitions: Political Empowerment for the 1990s*, ed. Roberto E. Villareal, Norma G. Hernandez, and Howard D. Neighbor. New York: Greenwood Press, 1991.

Saragoza, Alex. "Recent Chicano Historiography: An Interpretive Essay." *Aztlán* 19 (Spring, 1988–90): 1–78.

Saxton, Alexander. *The Rise and Fall of the White Republic: Class Politics and Mass Culture in Nineteenth-Century America*. New York: Verso, 1990.

Shockley, John. *Chicano Revolt in a Texas Town.* Notre Dame, Ind.: University of Notre Dame Press, 1974.

Shook, Robert. *Reflections on Old Victoria.* Victoria, Tex.: Robert Bennet Publishers, 1979.

Skerry, Peter. *Mexican Americans: The Ambivalent Minority.* New York: The Free Press, 1993.

Soukup, James, R, Clifton McCleskey, and Harry Holloway. *Party and Factional Division in Texas.* Austin: University of Texas Press, 1964.

Stewart, Kenneth L., and Arnoldo De León. *Not Room Enough: Mexicans, Anglos, and Socioeconomic Change in Texas, 1850–1900.* Albuquerque: University of New Mexico Press, 1993.

Taylor, Paul S. *An American-Mexican Frontier: Nueces County, Texas.* New York: Russell and Russell, 1971.

———. *Mexican Labor in the United States: Dimmit County, Winter Garden District, South Texas.* University of California Publications in Economics. Vol. 6, No. 5. Los Angeles: University of California Press, 1930.

Texas Good Neighbor Commission. *Texas: Friend and Neighbor.* Austin: Von Boeckmann-Jones Press, 1961.

Thernstrom, Stephan, ed. *Harvard Encyclopedia of American Ethnic Groups.* Cambridge: Harvard University Press, 1980.

Thompson, Jerry D. *Mexican Texans in the Union Army.* El Paso: Texas Western Press, 1986.

———. *Vaqueros in Blue and Gray.* Austin: Presidial Press, 1976.

Treviño, Roberto R. *"La Fe: Catholicism and Mexican Americans in Houston, 1911–1972."* Ph.D. diss., Stanford University, 1993.

Tyler, Ronnie C., et al., eds. *The New Handbook of Texas.* 6 Vols. Austin: Texas State Historical Association, 1996.

Urbano, David. "The Saga of a Revolutionary Family: The Martín de León Family of Texas." Master's thesis, University of Texas, San Antonio, 1990.

Valenzuela, Angela. *Subtractive Schooling: U.S.-Mexican Youth and the Politics of Caring.* Albany: State University of New York Press, 1999.

Villareal, Roberto E. "The Politics of Mexican-American Empowerment," 1–7. In *Latino Empowerment: Progress, Problems, and Prospects,* ed. Roberto E. Villareal, Norma G. Hernandez, and Howard D. Neighbor. New York: Greenwood Press, 1988.

Villareal, Roberto E., Norma G. Hernandez, and Howard D. Neighbor, eds. *Latinos and Political Coalitions: Political Empowerment for the 1990s.* New York: Greenwood Press, 1991.

"Walking Humbly in Victoria." *Revista Maryknoll* 10 (October, 1984): 2–8.

Weber, David J. *Foreigners in Their Native Land: Historical Roots of the Mexican Americans.* Albuquerque: University of New Mexico Press, 1973.

Whitaker, Theora. *Victoria.* Victoria, Tex.: *Victoria Advocate* Publishing Company, 1941.

Zamora, Emilio. *The World of the Mexican Worker in Texas.* College Station: Texas A&M University Press, 1993.

Index

Page numbers in *italic* type refer to illustrations

Abilene, Kansas, 10
accommodation, 77, 103
acculturation of Mexican Americans, 27
Acevedo, Rev. Cayetano, 55
ACLU (American Civil Liberties
    Union), 56
ACSC (American Citizens' Social
    Club), 77–85, 94, 97, 101, 103, 104, 123
ACSCI (American Citizens' Social Club
    Incorporated), 84
ACWA (Amalgamated Clothing Workers
    of America), 78, 88–90, 127
Adams, Aquilla, 73
AFDC (Aid to Families with Dependent
    Children), 112
AFL-CIO, 89
African Americans: as freedmen, 7; in
    contrast to Mexican Americans, ix–x;
    occupations of 14
AGIF (American G. I. Forum), 23, 35,
    56, 57, 78, 85–88, 94, 97, 101, 103, 104,
    106, 123, 127; Ladies Auxiliary, 86
agricultural production, 12. *See also* cot-
    ton production
ALCOA (Aluminum Company of Amer-
    ica), 17
Alinsky, Saul, 46, 78
Allred, James V., 104
American society, structure of, xv
Anglo Americans: as friends, ix; coexis-
    tence with, xii
Anglo domination: Mexican American
    challenges to, xix; of society, 3
anti-communism, xvi

Aransas County, Texas, 10
Armstrong, A. Willis, 111, 113, 114, 116
Artero, John, 60, 70, 71, 76, 102, 104
assimilation: goals of, xi; of Mexican
    Americans, 126; of the author, x
at-large electoral structure. *See* voting
attitudes: Anglos toward Mexicans, ix, x,
    6, 7, 8, 9, 10, 14, 22; in public schools,
    50, 56; Mexican Americans toward
    government, 63

Baass, Alfred, 119
Ballet Folklorico, 36–41, 126
Barrio, 19
Bastrop Independent School District
    (BISD), 57
Beall's Department Store, 89
Benavides, Plácido, 5
Benavides, Ysidore, 8
Bennett, Stephen, 74–75
Bentson, Lloyd, 62
bicultural identity. *See* identity
black bean incident, 8
Black Legend, 7
blacks. *See* African Americans
Blanton, Annie Webb, 52
"blowouts," 107
Bonilla, Rubén, 92, 95
Borrego, Alfred, 86
Boy's Club, 96
Bravo, Manuel, 100
Breech, Gary, 123
Briscoe, Dolph, 109–10
Brown, J. E. "Buster," 122

Brown v. Board of Education, 50, 58
Bryant, Vaughn, 20

CAC (Citizens' Advisory Committee), 113
Callis, C. R., 63
Camargo, Mexico, 8
Cameron County, 100
Cano, Jesse, 115
Cano, Martín, 61, 102, 107
Cantú, Pete, 84, 111, 112, 115
capitalism, rejection of, xi
Carbajal, José M. 5
Care Inn South, 91–92
Carsner, C. C., 113, 114, 116
Castillo, Ralph, 84
Catholic church, xxiv; Catholic faith,
    24; Mexican and Mexican American
    Catholics, 14; relationship to Mexican
    Americans, xxiv, 25, 33; vehicle for
    expression of identity, 44
Catholicism, 126
Catholic Southwest, xiii
Catholic War Veterans, 35–36, 47;
    Ladies Auxiliary, 36
Catholic Youth Organization, 36–41, 47,
    48, 126
cattle. *See* ranching
CCD (Confraternity of Christian Doc-
    trine), 45
Centralist party of Mexico, 5
Chamber of Commerce, 88
Chandler, C. O., 62, 63
Charter Revision Committee of Victoria,
    114
Chávez, César, xix, 105
Chicanismo, xxv, 43
Chicano generation, 106
Chicano movement, xvii, xxii, 105
Christianity, xvii
citizens, "acceptable and unacceptable",
    10

Citizens' Advisory Committee. *See* CAC
Citizenship: definition of, x; ideological
    components of, xii, xvi; mainstream
    definitions of, x, xvi, xvii, xxi, 3, 48;
    Mexican American definitions of, xv,
    xvii–xix, xxiii, 87; requirements of, xi
Civil Rights Act of 1964, 61, 75
civil rights movement: xvi
Civil War, 11
class: distinctions, 13; lack of conscious-
    ness among Mexican Americans, xviii,
    xx, xxv
Club Westerner, 21
Cold War, effects on definitions of citi-
    zenship, xvi
Colella, Father David, 46
Coleman, James, Jr., 113
Colorado, battleship, 34
color blind society, xi
communism, xvi; fear of subversion, 3
Confraternity of Christian Doctrine.
    See CCD
Conjunto. *See* music
consensualism, xix, xx, xxii, xvii–xviii
consumerism, xvi
corn production, 12
Corpus Christi, Texas, 11, 45, 69, 117
Corpus Christi Caller Times, 108
Cós, Martin Perfecto de, 5
cotton production, 10, 12
Council of Defense, 15
Cox, Judge Owen D., 66, 69, 119
Crain Jr. High School, 60, 61
Crimm, Ana Carolina Castillo, 7
Criollo, 17
cross-class consensus, xviii
Crystal City, Texas, 106
Cuero, Texas, 11
culture, Mexican American, xxi
cultural deficiencies among Mexican
    Americans, 27

Cursillo, 42, 47
Czechoslovakian immigrants, 24

Dabney, Jean, 91
Dallas, Texas, 47
Daniel, Price, 57
Davis, Arnold, 72
Dawson, Roger, 111
DeAnda, James, 57
Declaration of Indpendence, 23
DeLeón club, 78, 95–98
DeLeón, Félix, 17
DeLeón, Fernando, 5
DeLeón, Martín, 4, 17, 24; empresario
    colony, 4; family, 6
DeLeón, Silvestre, 5
DeLeón, Wence, 116
Delgado, Carlos, 54–56
Delgado, Daniel, 88
Del Rio, Anita, 94
democracy, 41
Democratic Party, 99, 120, 121, 123, 124
Department of Justice, 71–72
Diez y seis de Septiembre, 107
discrimination: housing, 22; employ-
    ment, 22; gender 36
Dobie, J. Frank, 8
Dudley Elementary School, 64
Dukakis, Michael, 124
Dunlap's, 89
DuPont plant. *See* E. I. DuPont de
    Nemours and Co.

economic mobility for Mexican Ameri-
    cans, 16–17
education, xviii; American Citizens'
    Social Club efforts, 83; goals of, 50,
    52, 53; as mirror of society, 51
egalitarianism, xv
E. I. DuPont de Nemours and Co., 18
Elizondo, Paul, 96

El grito de Dorlores, 107
el movimiento, xxv
El Paso, Texas, 88, 89, 110, 125
empresario communities, 3
English language, x, 15
Equal Employment Opportunity Com-
    mission (EEOC), 65

Fagan, Mary, 10
"family values," 124
Farah company, the, 88
farming, 13, 18
fascism, xvi
Fieles de Burgos, 4
Fifth Circuit Court of Appeals, 119
Flores, Archbishop Patrick, 45, 46
Flores, Beatrice, 63
Ft. Bliss, 107
Ft. Worth, Texas, 11
Foster Field, 19, 20
Fourteenth Amendment, 57
Fury, Archbishop Francis J., 46

Galvan, Eddie, 96
Galvan, Willie, 115
García, Cristobal, 65–66, 69–70, 93
García, Gus, 57
García, Hector P., 85, 87
García, Mario, T., xx, 17
Garrett, Jerry, 120
GCOE (Gulf Coast Organizing Effort),
    46–48
Gee, Roger, 63, 65
gender discrimination. *See*
    discrimination
German: Americans 12, 17; immigrants,
    15, 24; Lutherans, 16
G. I. generation, 79, 105
Giorgi, Reverend Daniel E., 29, 30, 32
Golden Crescent, 18, 46, 127

Goliad, Texas, 9, 10
Gonzáles, Gil, 123
Gonzáles, Nicole Jeanine, 38
Gonzáles, Rodolfo "Corky," xix, 105
González, Beatríz Quintanilla, 119, 120
González, Gilbert, 51
González, Henry, 82
Good Neighbor Commission, 20;
    Human Relations Council of, 21
Grahmann, Archbishop David, 45, 46,
    47
Gray, Mabry "Mustang," 8
greaser, x
Great Depression, 16, 17
Green, Sam, Jr., 111
Gross Elementary, 64
Grover, Henry, 109
Guadalupanas, 33–34, 37
Guadalupe river, 3, 4, 12
Guadalupe school (Catholic), 27
Guadalupe school (public), 60, 61
Guadalupe Valley Railroad, 11
Guadalupe Victoria, 5
Guerra, Manuel, 100
Gutiérrez, José Angel, xix, 109
Gutiérrez, Teresa, 70–72; 74–76
Gutiérrez, Wenceslao, 75

Hacheros, los. *See* Woodsmen of the
    World
Hallettsville, Texas, 46
Hallettsville Highway, 13
Hammett, A. B. J., 6
Hanley, Charles, 116
Harris, Dwight, 75
Harrison County, Texas, 11
Health Education and Welfare Depart-
    ment (HEW), 61, 62, 65, 114
Heck, Father F. X., 26, 28, 29
Hemmis, Patsy, 40, 41, 48
highways, 13
Hijas de Maria, Las, 33

Hinojosa, Gilberto, 43
Hinojosa, Nick, 102, 117–18, 119
hispanic, xxii
Hobbs, R. E. Gene, 112, 113
Holzheauzer, Steve, 122–23
Hoover, J. Edgar, 87
Hopkins School, 60, 61, 64, 111
House Un-American Activities Commit-
    tee (HUAC), 87
Houston, Sam, 6, 8; street, 13
Houston, Texas, 11, 125
Houston Post, 20
Huelga, 107
Human Relations Council. *See* Good
    Neighbor Commission
Huvar, Val, 120

Idar, Ed, 20
identity: Anglo American, xxii; as citi-
    zens, xxi, 86–88, 97, 99; bicultural
    nature of, xii, 17, 23, 39, 40, 106
ideology: of Mexican Americans, xx;
    racial, 19
Indianola, Texas, 11
Industrial Areas Foundation, 46
industrialization in Victoria area, 22
inheritance practices, 7
integration, 56
International Union of Mine Mill and
    Smelter Workers, 87
Irish immigrants, 5, 12, 14, 24
Italian immigrants, 11, 24, 26

Jackson, Lullis, 115
Jaime, Alfredo, 115
Juan Linn School, 64, 111

Keeran, John Newbanks, 11
Kelly, Father Joseph, 45
Kleiber, Erskine, 117
Koontz, Henry Clay, 11
Koreneck, Sister Odelia, 46

La Bahia, 5
la causa, 107
land loss, 6
Laredo, Texas, 104
LaSalle County, 10
Las Cruces, New Mexico, 89
League of United Latin American Citizens, xvii, 16, 17, 23, 35, 56, 57, 69, 76, 78, 106, 115, 123, 127; Council 626, 90–92; Council 4319, 92–95, 97–98
League of Women Voters, 113, 114, 115
Ledesma, Lydia Serrata, 115, 116
Lentz, Cody, 22
Lentz, Zack, 22
Leuschner, Charles, A., 54
Linn, John J., 4, 5
Lockwood, Reverend James T., 30, 32
López, Matt, 83–84, 123
Los Angeles, California, 125
loyal opposition, xi
Lucey, Archbishop Robert E., 29, 32, 45, 46
Luera, Hildo, 111–12, 115, 121, 122
Luna, Alex, 115

"Macaroni line" railroad, 12
McCarthyism, 101
McFaddin: James, 11; ranch, 18
McGovern, George, 124
McHenry, John, 5
McMullen County, 10
mainstream: culture, xvi; ideology, xviii
Main Street, 12
managers, 14
Marquez, Benjamin, 94
Martínez, Roque "Rocky," 91, 94
Martínez, Sister Stephanie Marie, 46
mass culture, xvi
Melvin's Globe Clothiers, 89
Méndez, Gonzalo, 56
"Meskin," x, ix
Mestizo. *See* Mexican American

Mexican: "bad," x, 9; "good," x; attitudes toward, 14; as immigrants, 26
Mexican American: as second-class citizen, xi, xv; consciousness, xix, 32; culture, 37, 39; generation, xxi; identity, xvii, xxii; identity as mestizos, 18; in contrast to African Americans, x; labor, 51; land ownership, 7; middle class, 13, 124, 126; professional class, xii, xviii–xix, 126; quest for public legitimacy, xii; social marginalization of, 12; struggles for citizenship, xi; values, xvii; views of American society, xxii; working class, 126
Mexican American Chamber of Commerce, 72
Mexican American Legal Defense and Education Fund (MALDEF), 70–71, 73–76, 118
Mexican American Political Association (MAPA), 104
Mexican American Youth Organization (MAYO), 108
Mexican Constitution of 1824, 5
Mexican school, 55–56
Mexican War, 14
Mexico City, 38, 39
middle class, ix, x
Midwest United States, 15
Mier expedition, 8
Milwaukee, Wisconsin, 34
Mine Mill. *See* International Union of Mine Mill and Smelter Workers
Mission Dolores, 24, 27
Missouri Pacific, 13
Mitchell school, 64
mob action, 9, 10
modernization in agriculture, 12
Mondale, Walter, 124
Moody Street, 12
Morán, Oscar, 95
Moya, Antonio, 10

Moya, Juan, 9
Moya, Marcelo, 9
Muñiz, Ramsey, 108–10
music, 96
mutualistas, 97

National Association for the Advance-
    ment of Colored People (NAACP), 92,
    113, 115
National Labor Relations Board
    (NLRB), 89
nationalism, 79, 124
nativism, 14, 124
Navarro, Armando, xix
Navarro Street, 13
Nazareth Academy, 27
neo-conservatism, 121
New Deal, 124
New Orleans, Louisisana, 119
New York, Texas and Mexican Rail-
    road, 11
Nixon, President Richard M., 39, 62
Nobles, Jerry, 120, 121
Northeast United States, 15
North Street, 12

Obledo, Mario, 95
Ochoa, Beatrice, 115
O'Connor, family, 24
O'Connor, Thomas, 10, 11
Olmstead, Frederick Law, 9
Opelousas, Louisiana, 6
Order of Sons of America, xvii
otherness, xxiii
Our Lady of Guadalupe, 26
Our Lady of Lourdes (Catholic Church),
    24
Our Lady of Sorrows (Catholic Church),
    24, 27, 28, 30, 78, 107
Ozuna, Isidore, 34

Pacheco, Manuel, 93
Padilla, Carlos, 116

Panic of 1873, 11
Patrizi, Father Vincent, 37, 39; attempts
    to oust, 44–45
Patti Welder Jr. High School, 60, 61, 111
Peña, Joe, 102, 116–17
Petrochemical industry, 19
Phillips, Oscar, 104, 115
Placedo, Texas, 81
Pleasure Island: centennial celebration,
    17; segregation, 17, 21–22
Political Association of Spanish Speak-
    ing Organizations (PASSO), 104
political: disenfranchisement, 100; en-
    franchisement, xxiv; hegemony by
    Anglos, 12; participation by Mexican
    Americans, xviii
Political machines, 100
Poll tax. *See* voting
Polzin, Don, 112
popular culture, as hegemonic, x
Population: growth of 3, 19, 22; physical
    dispersion of, 13
Port Lavaca, Texas, 11, 21, 81, 94
Power, James, 6, 10
Power-Hewetson colony, 10
prejudice, racial, 41
Pro, Noe, 96
professionalization, uplifting aspects
    of, xix
protestants, 24; capitalist culture, xxii
Pueyo, Reverend, 29, 30

Quadregsimo Ano, 45
Queen City, 13

race implications for citizenship, 16
racial harmony, 3, 5, 12
racism, x
radicalism, resistance to, xii, xviii, 41
Ramirez, Fausto, 20
Ranching, Brahman, 11; industry, 10,
    13, 18

Raza Unida party, xxv, 105, 108, 109, 110
Reed, Ted B., 113
reform, approaches to, xx
Refugio, Texas: county of 10, town of 8, 9
Republican Party, 99, 120, 121, 122
Rerum Novarum, 45
residential arrangements, 13
resistance, xix, 77
Reyna, Joseph E., 75
Rib's Café, 21
Rice, Judge Ben, 57
Rio Grande Street, 13
Rio Grande Valley, 42
Rivera, Chris, 72
Robles, Lupe, 30
Rodriguez, Jimmy, 107
Rojas, Alex, 72, 75, 115, 116
Rojas, Beatrice, 81
Rojas, Ralph, Sr., 80
Rojas, Ralph, Jr., 80
Rosati, Father Hyacinth, 37
Rosenberg, Texas, 11

St. Francis (Catholic Church), 26
St. Mary's (Catholic Church), 24, 26
Salazar, Rubén, 107
Salinas, J. E. D., 104
Saltillio, Coahua, Mexico, xv
Samuelson, Eric, 120
San Benito, Texas, 26
San Antonio and Mexican Gulf Railway, 11
San Antonio, Texas, 42, 46, 47, 88, 125
San Diego, California, 57
San Jacinto, battle of, 6, 10
San Patricio County, 10
Santa Anna, Antonio Lopez de, 5, 7
Saragoza, Alex, xx
Saunders, George, 10
Seadrift, Texas, 18
Segregation, 49; end of de jure in Victoria, 59; in public schools, 51

Seguin, Texas, 49
Seiler, W. L., 21
Sepveda, Elizabeth, 37
Sepveda, Pete, 37
Shaw, Reverend J. W., 26, 28, 29
Shepperd, Ben, 22
Single Member Districts. *See* voting
Sklar, Guthrie, 118
Smith Elementary School, 60, 61
Spanish language, abandonment of, x
socialism, xvii
social justice, xvi
social order, place of Mexican American in, x
Solís, Carlos, xv, 83
Somervell, Alexander, 8
southeast side, 13
Southern Pacific Railroad, 12
south side, 12
South Texas Studies, xiii
Southwestern Historical Quarterly, xiii
Southwestern Voter Research and Educational Project (SWVREP), 118, 119
Stanly Elementary school, 111
Starr County, 100
Steele, Charlie, 113
Stroman High School, 107
Summer Youth Recreation Program, 112
Supreme Court, 61
Swift family murder, 9

Targac, Frank, 118
Tejano, xi, 6, 12
Texas Department of Human Resources (TDHR), 91
Texas Education Agency (TEA), 65
Texas Revolution, 5, 12, 14, 24, 49
Texians, xxi, 12
Tijerina, Reies López, xix
Tivoli, Texas, 81
Torres, Rene, 122

totalitarianism, 36
Triangle Drive-in, 21

Union Carbide, 18, 19
United Citizens' Social Club, 85
United States Constitution, 23
University of Houston–Downtown, 93
University of Houston–Victoria, 96, 98
Urrea, José, 5
"us versus them," as an interpretive
　model, xx
Uthoff, Harry, 64, 65, 66

Vatican II, 43
Vaugn, Larry, 74
Vela Perpetua, 33
Velasco, Manuel, 59, 76, 101–104
Velasquez, Juan, 119, 120, 121
victimization, xix, xx
Victoria, Guadalupe (first President of
　Mexico), 4
Victoria, Texas, x; central portion of, 13;
　origins of, 3; post-revolution changes,
　6; hostile to Mexicans, 4; as home to
　chemical plant labor, 18; as home to
　author, xi; Chamber of Commerce,
　20; Housing Authority, 20, 21
Victoria Advocate, 72, 108
Victoria College, 85, 107
Victoria County Hispanics for Bush, 122
Victoria Independent School District
　(VISD), 58, 61, 62, 74–75; school
　board, 104; spending on minorities,
　58
Victorians: in black bean incident, 8;
　as nationalists, 15
Villa, Ramón, 108

*Villa de Nuestra Señorade Guadalupe
　Victoria Nombre de Jesús*, 4
Viva Kennedy, 81, 104
voting: at-large, 50, 60, 70; behavior of
　Mexican Americans, 100; polarized
　nature of, 60; poll taxes, 100; poll tax
　drives, 82, 101; Single Member Dis-
　tricts (SMDs), 115, 116
Voting Rights Act of 1965, 71, 100

Waco, Texas, 42
Walker, Helen, 120
Ware, Joseph, 4
Warren, Ed, 113
Water Street, 12
Welder: family 24; Dolores, 26; Frank,
　26, 27; John James, 11
Wells, Jame, 100
West Street, 12
Wexford County Ireland, 10
whiteness, xxii
white society, xi
William Offer school, 75
Wilson, Johnny, 74–75
Wood School, 60
Woodsmen of the World, 80
World War I, 49; and treatment of Ger-
　man Americans, 15–16; ideological
　impact of, 16
World War II: post-war ideology, xv, xvii,
　23
Wright, John D., 4

Yarbrough, Ralph, 82

Zapata County, 100
Zuber, Father, 28, 29, 30

CPSIA information can be obtained
at www.ICGtesting.com
Printed in the USA
LVHW03s1240020918
588933LV00002B/541/P